What's Cooking in Belgium

NEIL EVANS
ANNA JENKINSON

What's Cooking in Belgium

RECIPES AND STORIES
FROM A FOOD-LOVING NATION

Contents

Introduction

BELGIUM IS A FOOD-OBSESSED COUNTRY. THERE'S NO OTHER WAY of putting it. This is a nation that has associations to defend the traditions of every food imaginable, where produce markets spring up on almost every town square, and where bakers, butchers and fishmongers are still dearly cherished. Belgians are a people who love their local products and are proud of their regional specialities no matter whether they're prepared in a Michelin-starred restaurant or at home.

In writing this book, our aim is to share with you some of this Belgian pride and dispel the myth that Belgium is just about chocolate, beer and Brussels sprouts. These ingredients do of course play a role, but there are so many others that deserve a mention too: mussels, grey shrimps, chicory, asparagus, wild boar, minced meat, nutmeg, cinnamon... the list goes on.

Our research took us from the North Sea coast in the West to the Ardennes forest in the East as we criss-crossed the country talking to chefs, restaurant owners and market-stall holders, tourist offices, curators and book collectors in an effort to gain as many different perspectives on Belgian food as possible.

The result is a compilation of recipes and stories, with each chapter focusing on one particular theme, for example seafood, cheese or fruit; together they tell the story of Belgium and its love of food. For some readers, the book will live in the kitchen, for others on the coffee table. Maybe it will inspire you to discover new dishes, cook with new ingredients or travel around Belgium and try out local specialties. However you decide to use the book, we hope it will deepen your understanding of Belgian culinary culture.

CHOOSING THE DISHES

When we embarked on the project, there were friends who raised a sceptical eyebrow as to whether we would find enough Belgian recipes to fill a book. In fact, the difficulty was choosing which ones to include and which ones we would have to leave out. In each case, our guiding principles have been: which recipes best reflect the different aspects of Belgian cuisine and which recipes will our readers most enjoy eating?

In Belgium there is no one definitive version of a particular recipe. Everyone claims that theirs is the most authentic and that the one from the neighbouring town pales in comparison. It is really quite surprising how one dish can vary so much from one village to the next and even from one family to the next. As recipes have been passed down the generations, the essence of the dish has remained the same, but each cook has added his or her personal touch.

Neil – the cook in our book partnership – is no exception to this rule. Some of the recipes were passed down to him by his Belgian grandmother, while others have their origins in his extensive collection of Belgian cookbooks dating back more than 100 years; they have all been developed and discussed, tested and tasted with friends, colleagues and chefs.

Illustrating the recipes are beautiful photographs, for which we have the food stylist Hilde Oeyen and the photographer Diane Hendrikx to thank. We feel that the images capture the style of our book perfectly and hope you agree.

TELLING THE STORY

As well as sharing recipes, we also wanted to include stories that highlight the central role that food plays in Belgian culture. Talk to any Belgian and the conversation will sooner or later come round to food: the meal they had with friends at the weekend, the cooking programme they watched on television or the foods they ate for a special occasion, be it a wedding, a Saint's Day or a local annual fair. Eating and drinking are quite simply bound up in almost every aspect of life.

Anna – the writer of the stories in this book – has aimed to capture this by taking the reader on a culinary tour round the country, highlighting regional products, local traditions and quirky facts. She weaves in the historical and geographical influences that have played their part in determining the cuisine of the country and brings the texts to life with personal insights and anecdotes.

BELGIAN BACKGROUND

While this book is not the place to recount the complexities of Belgian history, geography or politics, a bit of background will nonetheless help explain why the cuisine of Belgium is so diverse.

First of all, consider the country's size and location. Given that Belgium only covers an area of about 30,500 km² (in other words you can fit about eight Belgiums into the United Kingdom), you are never far from one of its neighbours: the Netherlands, Germany, Luxembourg and France. It's hardly surprising therefore that, in one way or another, they have all influenced the cooking of Belgium. A common quip about Belgian food is that it combines the finesse of French cuisine with the generous portions of the Germans!

Historically, foreign influences have been dominant. Before declaring independence in 1830, Belgium had had many different rulers including the French, the Spanish, the Austrians and the Dutch. As borders moved back and forth, the northern and southern parts of present-day Belgium were not always ruled by the same power, which partly explains the diversity of cultures from one region to another. These factors also help explain why this country of approximately 11 million people has three official languages: Dutch (or Flemish) spoken in Flanders in the north of the country, French in Wallonia in the south and German by a minority in the east.

Over the centuries, traders and explorers have also played their part in introducing foods from different parts of the world to this northern corner of Europe. The Spanish *conquistadors* for example brought potatoes and chocolate, while the bustling ports of Bruges in the late Middle Ages and Antwerp as of the 16th century were places where spices such as cinnamon, nutmeg and ginger as well as all sorts of other ingredients were exchanged.

It is all these influences that have come together and reinforced each other over the years to create the dishes that today we consider as typical Belgian cuisine.

DEFENDING TRADITION

Belgians are a people who enjoy keeping traditions alive, and all the more so if they involve eating and drinking. This is probably why the *confréries*, associations that defend culinary heritage and promote local specialities, are so widespread. Take for example the Brotherhood of the Geraardsbergen Mattentaart in Flanders (Het Broederschap van de Geraardsbergse Mattentaart), the Association of the Master Brewers and Distillers in Wallonia (Confrérie des Maîtres Brasseurs et Distillateurs de Wallonie) or the Order of the Bloempanch to defend a local blood sausage in Brussels.

Throughout Belgium, food is much more than just fuel for the body. It is a source of pride and pleasure. It is an integral part of life. It is a means of identity. The fields and the orchards, the rivers and the sea, the forests and the farms; they all provide the regional products used to create Belgium's traditional dishes. We hope that our book provides an insight into this rich culture, encouraging you to cook some Belgian dishes and learn more about this country that has been our home for many years.

Bon appétit!
Anna and Neil

Belgium

1   Horseback shrimp fishermen in Oostduinkerke

2   Hop shoots festival and guided tours in Poperinge

3   *Krakelingen* festival and *mattentaarten* in Geraardsbergen

4   Chicory museum and restaurant in Kampenhout

5   Elixir from Spa

6   *Couques* from Dinant

7   Brewery in Chimay

8   Saint-Hubert's day celebrations

Conversion chart

OVEN TEMPERATURES

CELSIUS (°C)	FAHRENHEIT (°F)	GAS MARK
165	325	3
180	350	4
200	400	6
220	425	7
240	465	9

WEIGHTS

G (GRAMS)	OZ (OUNCES)
25g	1oz
50g	2oz
100g	3.5oz
200g	7oz
250g	9oz

VOLUMES

1 tbsp (tablespoon) = 3 tsp (teaspoons)

ML (MILLILITRES)	FL OZ (FLUID OUNCES)/PINT	CUPS
5ml		1 tsp (teaspoon)
15ml	½ fl oz	1 tbsp (tablespoon)
30ml	1 fl oz	1/8 cup
60ml	2 fl oz	¼ cup
120ml	4 fl oz	½ cup
150ml	5 fl oz/ ¼ pint	2/3 cups
240ml	9 fl oz/ ½ pint	1 cup

YEAST

FRESH YEAST	INSTANT DRY YEAST	ACTIVE DRY YEAST
42g	14g	21g
(1 cube in Europe)	(2 sachets)	
21g	7g or 2 tsp	10g or 4 tsp
10g	3.5g or 1 tsp	5g or 2 tsp

(Due to rounding, all conversions are approximate.)

Starting off with shrimps

GREY SHRIMPS, KNOWN LOCALLY AS 'THE caviar of the North Sea', have a special place in Belgian hearts and on Belgian menus, with shrimp croquettes and tomatoes stuffed with shrimps among the most popular starters in the country.

The revered grey shrimps are mostly fished by boats off Zeebrugge, Nieuwpoort and Ostend as well as along the Dutch coast. In the Belgian coastal town of Oostduinkerke, the shrimp fishermen don't go out in boats but on horseback, keeping alive a tradition that dates back some 600 years. Sitting astride the large, working horses, the fishermen ride into the sea, dragging their nets behind them to catch the local delicacy. It is the only place in the world where this technique can still be seen.

Oostduinkerke is also home to an annual shrimp festival during the last weekend of June. The celebrations start with a religious service and a consecration of the sea, after which shrimp-fishing contests, frying fish and a shrimp festival parade are all on the agenda.

Time has not stood still in every respect though. Whereas in the past, grey shrimps caught off the Belgian coast would have been peeled nearby, today they are transported to north Africa to be peeled by cheaper labour and then flown back again for sale here. Such are the quirks of global trade.

That said there's nothing to stop you from peeling your own shrimps, and the advantages aren't just environmental. One culinary bonus is that you can use the leftovers to make a flavoursome fish stock. Or if you're enjoying a day trip at the coast, unpeeled shrimps fresh from the sea are a popular snack to accompany a glass of beer such as a local Rodenbach. Peeling your own shrimps one by one may seem a fiddly and time-consuming activity, but sometimes it's good to slow down, and the reward is immediate and oh so tasty.

TOMATOES AND CROQUETTES

The classic starter of tomatoes stuffed with shrimps (referred to as *tomates crevettes* by the Francophones and *tomaat garnaal* by the Flemish), is a simple dish but one that has stood the test of time. Traditionally, it was a dish for special family occasions, not least because of the high cost of shrimps. Today, they are much more affordable and therefore enjoyed much more frequently.

As for shrimp croquettes, it is the contrast between the crunchy breadcrumbs on the outside and the creamy shrimp mixture on the inside that makes them such a delight to eat. Served warm and sprinkled with fried parsley, they're hard to beat.

Of course not all starters are based on shrimps. In the croquettes department, another popular choice is cheese croquettes. And there are salads, including the coastal salad made with shrimps, lettuce, tomatoes, boiled eggs and a generous serving of Belgians' favourite condiment, mayonnaise. And soups, not least shrimp soup. Okay, maybe there's no getting around it: shrimps are a staple for traditional Belgian starters.

Stuffed
TOMATOES

2 servings

1 saucepan

2 bowls

30 minutes

4 large tomatoes

400g unpeeled

(or 200g peeled shrimps)

100g mayonnaise

1 lemon

1 large handful of parsley

Celery salt

Finely ground white pepper

— Using a sharp knife, mark a cross on the base of 4 big, firm tomatoes. Leave their green stems intact. Blanch the tomatoes by carefully placing them in boiling water for 15 seconds and then transfer them to a bowl of cold water. Dry the tomatoes and peel off their skin. Slice off their tops and set aside. Scoop out the seeds and discard them. Wet a finger, dip it into the celery salt and rub in the inside of the tomato cavity. Repeat with the pepper.

— For the shrimp filling, mix 200g of peeled shrimps together with 100g of mayonnaise [→ see the recipe on p.60], the juice of half a lemon and a large handful of finely chopped parsley. Generously fill the tomatoes with the mixture before putting their lids back on at an angle, like little hats. Decorate with a sprig of parsley, half a lemon cut into wedges and any remaining shrimps.

In Belgium, the shrimps are called *crevettes grises/grijze garnalen*, which literally means grey shrimps. In English, these are more often called brown, common, sand or bay shrimps. If these are unavailable, then the dish can also be made with prawns, crab meat, lobster, crayfish, clams or surimi.

Shrimp-stuffed tomatoes are traditionally served with a simple salad garnish. This can be made more substantial by adding a combination of the following: grated carrot, a few slices of pear, sprouted seeds, baby green peas, thinly sliced mushrooms, sweetcorn, lamb's lettuce and fresh coriander.

They can be covered in clingfilm and chilled in the fridge for a day.

SHRIMP
Croquettes

16-24 croquettes

1 saucepan

1 baking tray
(30x40cm)

2 small bowls

1 frying pan
(or deep-fat fryer)

Preparation:
20-40 minutes
Refrigeration: 2 hours
Cooking: 20 minutes

250g whole shrimps
(or 175g peeled shrimps)

75g flour

75g butter

500ml milk

1 tbsp tomato purée

2 eggs

150g breadcrumbs

100ml oil

2 sprigs of parsley

Salt & pepper

Paprika

— The shrimps are best bought whole as their heads and tails can be used to infuse the creamy béchamel with their rich flavour. If they are uncooked, boil them in half a litre of salty water for 5 minutes, until they go pink and then peel them. Pan-fry the shrimps' heads and tails for a few minutes before boiling them in the milk for 10 minutes with a tablespoon of tomato purée. Sieve well before use.

— To make the béchamel, melt 75g of butter in a saucepan then add 75g of flour and fry it in the butter for a minute over a low heat. Add the shrimp-flavoured milk a quarter at a time and whisk until the sauce is smooth. As the sauce thickens, continue stirring regularly. Cook until the sauce has the consistency of a thick paste, which should take 8-12 minutes. Turn off the heat and allow to cool. When it is no longer steaming when stirred, add 2 egg yolks, a pinch of salt and pepper, and the shrimps. You may also want to add a few spices: a pinch of paprika will accentuate the pinkness of the shrimps.

— Mix the shrimps into the béchamel and then pour into a greased baking tray, about 30cm×40cm, to a thickness of 2-3cm. Cover with clingfilm and chill in the fridge for a few hours until firm.

— Cut the raw croquette into pieces the size of a pack of playing cards, then dip in beaten egg white before rolling them in breadcrumbs. Avoid the temptation to load the croquettes with as many breadcrumbs as possible as this will make them oily and doughy.

— They are now ready to be pan or deep fat fried at 180°C until golden brown, then tapped down with a paper napkin to remove any excess oil.

Ⓘ Croquettes can be kept in the fridge for 24 hours or in the freezer for up to a month. If you are cooking chilled croquettes then it is advisable to put them in an oven at 180°C for 5 minutes after frying them in order to make sure that the filling is cooked through.

Ⓘ Croquettes are served with bread and a sprig of parsley that has been fried in hot oil for a minute. Shrimp croquettes are garnished with a wedge of lemon.

Ⓘ In many Belgian households, croquettes were traditionally made from the leftovers of the previous night's meal. In restaurants cheese croquettes are rectangular, meat croquettes like long, thin sausages and shrimp croquettes like short, fat sausages.

Travels around Wallonia

THE WALLOONS, THE FRENCH-SPEAKING BELGIANS WHO LIVE IN THE south of the country, pride themselves on their simple traditional food. While there is no one dish that represents Wallonia, what is common to almost all cuisine from this region is the use of local produce, be it cheese, butter and milk from the many dairy farms, trout from the rivers or game and smoked ham from the Ardennes forest.

The local dried ham known as *jambon d'Ardenne* [→ see also the section on pork, p.98) is a specialty that finds its way into many Walloon dishes, being added to winter soups, used in salads and chopped up into creamy sauces. Chunks of bacon, referred to locally as *lardons*, are another common addition such as in the sauce of Ardennes-style mussels or as a vital ingredient in a *salade Liègoise*, a warm salad from Liège.

The popularity of dairy products can be seen from the number of *tartes* in Wallonia. A tart in this part of the world can be savoury, somewhere between a quiche and a flan, or sweet, a cross between a cake and a pie. As for sweet tarts, Verviers' rice tart is one of the best known, the recipe and story for which are included in the desserts section [→ p.176]. On the savoury front, there is for example Nivelles' green *tarte al djote*, made with chard and a local cheese, and Dinant's *flamiche* made with another local cheese, eggs and butter. In Jodoigne, the local *tarte au fromage* – or *blanke doréye* in the Walloon dialect – is a cream cheese tart that has become inextricably linked with the town's culinary heritage.

While each part of Wallonia has a local product or dish for which it is renowned, Liège does seem to have more than most. Ask a French-speaking Belgian to name a traditional dish and *salade Liègoise* is likely to be high on the list, along with *boulets à la Liègeoise* [→ see recipe on p.120 for these Liège-style meatballs] and *gaufres de Liège* [→ see recipe on p.162 for these waffles]. Ask for a typical product used in Walloon cooking and the top answers would not only include beer, but also a thick fruit spread known as *sirop de Liège* [→ see also the section on fruit, p.164], made from the crop of the local orchards.

FÊTES DE WALLONIE

Each of these products, like so many others in the country, has a *confrérie*, which is an association of people who defend and promote their local specialties and associated traditions.

For an introduction to the Walloon *confréries*, a good starting point is the annual festival known as the Fêtes de Wallonie: as well as processions and general merrymaking, the region-wide festivities also place a lot of emphasis on eating and drinking. In some towns, local squares are filled with stands belonging to the different *confréries*, where the associations' members dress up in traditional costume and serve their specialty, often accompanied with the locals' favourite drink, *pèkèt* [→ see also the section on strong drinks, p.196].

The best place to celebrate the Fêtes de Wallonie is arguably the capital of Wallonia, Namur. Here there is a *confrérie* to safeguard the people of Namur's cultural traditions: its symbols are snails, a local delicacy, and pèkèt, almost a local institution. Namur, like other Walloon towns, is proud of its culinary heritage and is keen to pass on that pride to future generations.

Liège-style SALAD

4 servings

1 small saucepan
1 large saucepan
1 steamer
1 frying pan
1 small bowl
1 large heatproof salad
bowl for serving

Preparation: 10 minutes
Cooking: 30 minutes

500g green beans
(French beans or string beans)
600g waxy new potatoes
200g diced bacon
1 large onion
1 garlic clove
2 tbsp chicken stock or water
4 tbsp vinegar
4 tbsp olive oil
1 handful of parsley
1 handful of celery
(or lovage leaves)

— Prepare the green beans by washing, topping and tailing them, and cutting any long ones in halfs or thirds. Peel the potatoes and boil in salted water for 20 minutes. Slice the onion into half rings and set aside. Crush a clove of garlic and mix it in a small bowl with a couple of tablespoons of olive oil. When the potatoes have been boiling for 5-10 minutes, steam the beans above them, or cook with a cup of water in a separate pan.

— Fry the diced bacon (sold as *lardons* or *spekblokjes* in Belgium) in a little oil until crisp, then set aside. You must now decide whether you want to serve the dish with raw or fried onions, or a mixture of the two. If frying, do this in the bacon fat until they brown, then return the bacon to the pan to heat through. If serving raw onions, chop the half rings into much small pieces.

— When the beans are al dente, remove them and rinse under cold water for 10 seconds, which is long enough to stop them cooking whilst ensuring they remain warm. Set aside under a lid. When the potatoes are cooked, remove them from the pan and cut them into ½-1cm thick slices. Use the cooking water to heat the large heatproof salad bowl that will be used to serve the dish.

— Rub the garlic-oil mix into the sides of the warm salad bowl and add the potatoes. Cover with the green beans, warm bacon, onions and celery or lovage leaves. Cover the salad bowl while you make the sauce, by deglazing the hot frying pan with a couple of tablespoons of chicken stock or water and 4 tablespoons of vinegar. Turn the heat up high and let the liquids boil as you scrape the bacon oil and onion sugars off the bottom of the pan. Pour over the salad, add a handful of chopped parsley and serve warm.

The secret to a successful *salade Liègoise* is good quality vinegar. Sherry vinegar with an acetic acid level of 8% is best. Alternatively use red or white wine vinegar. If this has a lower acid level then replace one of the tablespoons with strong white vinegar.

Waxy potatoes lend themselves well to this dish; in Belgium, the Corne de Gatte variety is the most highly regarded.

Pea & ham SOUP

⫯⫯ 4 servings

✐ 1 large saucepan

   1 bowl

   1 blender

🕑 Preparation: 30 minutes

   Cooking: 60 minutes

300g fresh or frozen peas

1 small onion

2 sticks of celery

1 small leek

2 potatoes

250g pork belly, knuckle

(or chunk of dried ham)

A splash of oil

1 ½ litres water

OPTIONAL:

250ml milk

— Fry a roughly chopped onion, 2 sticks of celery and a small leek in a splash of oil for 10 minutes. Transfer to a saucepan and add the peas, 2 peeled potatoes, 1½ litres of water and the pork meat. It is best not to cut the meat up as it will need to be retrieved from the pot after cooking. Smoked meats will give a rougher, earthier taste to the dish.

— Simmer with the lid on over a low heat for an hour. Stir and skim the froth off the surface occasionally.

— When cooked, remove the meat and use a blender to turn the liquid and vegetables into a smooth soup. If it is too thick then it can be thinned with a cup of milk. Return to a low heat whilst you chop up the pork into small pieces and add them back to the soup. Be sure not to let the soup boil as this will spoil the dish's vibrant colour and delicate flavour.

Serve with croutons and crusty brown bread.

This soup was traditionally cooked with the bone and dry, tough offcuts of an Ardennes ham, and fresh peas were used in the summer and dried peas out of season. If you use dried peas, soak 150g of whole or split peas in 1½ litres of water overnight, and use this flavour-rich water to make the soup.

Down by
the river

ONE OF THE MOST POPULAR FRESHWATER FISH IN BELGIUM IS TROUT, and one Belgian village that takes its trout very seriously is Ligneuville in the Ardennes. Nicknamed the 'Trout Capital', Ligneuville is renowned for both its trout farms and trout fishing in the River Amblève that flows through the village.

The Amblève is of course not the only river where trout as well as other freshwater species such as carp and pike are fished. In the Ardennes there are also the Ourthe, the Semois and the Lhomme, while further west there are the Sambre and the Meuse, all of which are popular with fishing enthusiasts.

The Belgians have numerous ways of cooking their trout, including with dry-roasted almonds, using Ardennes ham and Ittre-style, using white wine vinegar [→ see recipe p.36]. They enjoy eating trout as a fillet, smoked or marinated, as well as turning it into potted fish, pâté or savoury mousse. The roe is also considered a delicacy, eaten as caviar on toast or as an accompaniment to a main dish.

The popularity of trout in Belgium is not exclusively due to its taste. It is also partly due to the declining stocks of other freshwater fish, some of which have all but disappeared from the country's rivers while others have become rare sights. *Waterzooi*, a Belgian dish that is part stew, part hearty soup, exemplifies this development: originally made with freshwater fish, *waterzooi* is today more commonly made with chicken [→ see p.137].

There are efforts both in Wallonia and Flanders to boost fish populations. In Flanders, money is being invested in fish farms and lakes to develop the region's aquaculture sector. Fish being bred include carp, sturgeon and trout. In Wallonia, Saumon-Meuse 2000 is a project focused on repopulating the river Meuse with salmon, a fish that migrates from the sea to the rivers to reproduce. In the 19th century salmon were a common sight in Wallonia, but industrialisation led to pollution and barriers being built along the rivers blocking the fish's path. As a result, the salmon slowly disappeared. In the 1980s, Saumon-Meuse 2000 was launched to improve the water quality, remove the obstacles and encourage salmon to reproduce in the Meuse; by the 21st century promising results were visible, not only for salmon but also other fish.

Many ways of cooking freshwater fish are as relevant for one type as for another. Take for example *escavèche*, a way of preparing fish that is said to have arrived in Belgium with the Spanish when they ruled this part of the world in the 16th century. While there are variations from one Walloon town to another, the key element to *escavèche*-style fish is the vinegar, which is used to marinate and preserve the fish.

EEL

The Belgians are also very fond of their eel. The most popular eel dish in the country is *paling in 't groen*, or eels in green sauce, taking its name from the bright green, chervil-based sauce that is served with the fish. Few Belgians prepare the dish themselves at home, preferring to buy it pre-prepared from the fishmonger or eating it in restaurants.

In the past, the eels were sourced in Belgium, particularly in and around the River Scheldt in Flanders; today, however, they are either imported or raised on eel farms.

European eel stocks have plummeted in recent years owing to pollution, loss of habitat and overfishing. As a result, in 2007 the European eel was listed as a protected species by CITES (Convention on International Trade in Endangered Species). How much longer eels remain on the menu will be determined by how well fish stocks and natural habitats can be protected.

Poached Ittre-style TROUT

2 servings

1 large frying pan

1 small saucepan

1 – 1½ hours

300-500g trout (or carp or pike)

250ml white wine

100ml white wine vinegar

2 small carrots

1 large onion

2 garlic cloves

2 slices lemon

1 sprig of thyme

1 sprig of tarragon

2 sprigs of parsley

2 bay leaves

2 cloves

1 tsp crushed coriander seeds

1 tsp mixed crushed white, black and red peppercorns

A generous pinch of salt

FOR THE SAUCE:

2 small shallots

100g mushrooms

1 large knob of butter

1 sprig of parsley

1 sprig of tarragon

— In a fish pan or deep frying pan, put 1 litre of water with the wine, onion (roughly chopped), carrots (cut into coins), garlic, lemon, salt, cloves, coriander, peppercorns, thyme, tarragon, parsley and bay leaves. Bring to the boil before simmering on a moderate heat for 20-45 minutes.

— When the stock is ready, wash the fish inside and out, and put it on a plate. Heat the white wine vinegar to near boiling in a microwave or small pan and pour over the fish. A tarragon-flavoured vinegar will enrich the character of the dish.

THE SAUCE:

— Fry a couple of thinly sliced shallots in butter until translucent. To these, add thinly sliced mushrooms and fry in a little more butter for 5 minutes. Shortly before cooking the fish, add 5 tablespoons of stock and a handful of finely chopped parsley and tarragon to the shallots and mushrooms. Give the pan a 45 second blast on a high heat, then put a lid on the saucepan and turn the heat off.

— Place the fish in the simmering stock. Cooking time will vary according to the size of the fish: a 25cm trout needs 8 minutes, whereas a bigger fish requires 12-15 minutes.

This dish can be served hot or cold. If served cold, the fish should be left to cool in the stock and the cooking time should be reduced by 4 minutes. When served cold, poached Ittre-style fish is often accompanied by fresh mayonnaise [→ see p.60] and a potato salad. When served hot, accompany with *stoemp* and a peppery, earthy salad made from a selection of lamb's lettuce, chicory, rocket, beans, walnuts, radishes, celery, currants, cucumber, shallots and a boiled egg.

FRIED TROUT
with almonds

2 servings

1 frying pan
2 small bowls

45 minutes

2 small trout (150-200g)
(or 1 larger fish (400-450g))
1 handful of sliced almonds
1 shallot
1 tbsp flour
2 handfuls of garden herbs
(e.g. coriander, dill, lemon
verbena, lemon thyme)
150ml white wine or cream
1 knob of butter
1 handful of parsley
2 tsp grated lemon
and orange zest
1 splash of oil
Celery salt
OPTIONAL:
¼ orange
½ lemon
Finely ground white pepper

— Open, empty and wash the fish, but don't rub off the outer layer of viscous mucus. The trout's head should not be removed before cooking (as there is exquisitely tender flesh in the cheeks) but the tail can be trimmed.

— Dry-roast the sliced almonds in the frying pan over a medium heat for 2 minutes. Set aside. Add the oil to the pan and fry a finely chopped shallot until soft and clear.

— Rub a little pepper and celery salt into the internal cavity of the fish and cover the outside with flour. It can then be filled with a mix of garden herbs and other fresh-flavoured plants such as a slice of lemon, a thinly cut stick of rhubarb, lemongrass or a couple of raspberries. A toothpick or two will close the cavity.

— The fish should be fried in a mix of oil and butter, over a medium heat. They will take 4-8 minutes per side depending on the size. If the fish is very large then scoring the flesh along the dorsal bone on the side where the flesh is thickest will even out its cooking. Try to turn it just once in the pan using a large spatula.

— Once the fish is cooked, set it aside on a plate under a low grill or covered in tinfoil while you prepare the sauce in the hot pan that was used to cook the fish. Deglaze the pan (scrapping the sediment and sugars off the bottom) with half a glass of white wine or cream. Add the fried shallot. Cook through on a low heat for 2 minutes. Add the butter, a small knob at a time. Take the pan off the heat and add the parsley and the citrus zest. If you've used white wine, add the juice of a quarter of an orange and half a lemon. With cream, add a pinch of finely ground white pepper.

— Serve the fried trout onto warm plates with the dry roast almonds sprinkled over the fish and sauce.

ⓘ Traditionally, this dish is served with broccoli *stoemp*, or buttered boiled potatoes dressed with finely chopped parsley and mint. A crunchy salad made of a mix of lettuce, coriander leaves, watercress, sweetcorn, beetroot, fennel and radishes also accompanies this well.

Along the North Sea coast

BELGIUM'S COASTLINE MAY ONLY BE 67 kilometres (42 miles) long, but it has a strong influence on the country, its people and its food. Belgians love going to their coast, which takes in the ports of Zeebrugge, Ostend and Nieuwpoort as it runs from the Netherlands in the north to France in the south.

Dotted all along the North Sea coast are seafood restaurants, fishmongers and open-air stands, offering everything from seafood elegantly served in Michelin-starred luxury to a traditional fish *waterzooi* in a more affordable restaurant or simply a tub of whelks to be enjoyed walking along the promenade.

In days gone by, the catch would have been shipped directly inland and brought ashore in places such as St. Catherine's square in Brussels, an area that to this day has maintained its reputation as the capital's fish district. Today, the fish caught in the North Sea are rarely shipped further than coastal towns such as Zeebrugge, where they are sold at auction, sometimes staying in Belgium, often being exported.

So which types of fish and seafood do Belgians particularly like to eat? Shrimps, crabs, lobsters and whelks, which live close to the Belgian shoreline where the sea is shallow and the seabed covered in sand and gravel, are all local favourites.

As for fish, one of the most popular types is undoubtedly sole, which represents about half of the gross earnings of the Belgian fishery fleet. Sea fishing also supplies the country with the likes of plaice, herring and cod.

A CHANGING INDUSTRY

Cod is a well-loved fish, but also one that reflects changes that have taken place in the fishing industry in recent years, where bigger boats, bigger fleets and bigger nets have all contributed to overfishing, higher consumption and reduced stocks. In the case of cod, the overfishing of the Atlantic variety means that vessels now go as far as the Arctic to find more abundant stocks.

There have also been many other changes in the species found and fished. Skate used to be cheap; now some species are listed as vulnerable or endangered. Eels used to be a food for the poor; now they are expensive and often imported. Gurnard was once an unwanted part of the catch, cast aside or sold for bait; now this fish (particularly red gurnard) is increasingly sold in fishmongers and is being strongly promoted.

Changing environments and changing habits have shaped the story of fish in Belgium, as elsewhere. Nonetheless, the Belgian coast still supports a fishing industry and the North Sea remains the source of many locals' livelihoods.

[→ For more about grey shrimps, please turn to 'Starting off with shrimps' on p.16, and for mussels, 'Mussels and chips' on p.50.]

SOLE
meunière

2 servings

2 frying pans
(1 per fish)

Preparation: 15 minutes
Cooking: 10 minutes

2 sole

2 lemons

50g flour

8 tbsp sunflower oil

100g butter

1 handful of parsley

Salt & pepper

OPTIONAL:

2 tbsp capers

—— Begin by choosing a good quality fish: a large sole, weighing more than 300g, over 30cm long and bearing the Marine Stewardship Council (MSC) ecolabel. Unlike other fish, which are best fresh out of the sea, sole's unique flavour develops in the muscle tissue 2-3 days after it has been caught. However don't let that be an excuse for a fishmonger to sell you an inferior product: look for the telltale signs of a flat fish's freshness, which are the smell and the brightness of the eyes. A fish in prime condition smells of seaweed, iodine and the sea and has glassy eyes.

—— Prepare the fish for the pan by carefully washing the fish inside and out, using the handle of a spoon to clean the internal cavity. Cut off the gills and the long fins that run along both sides with scissors. Repeat with the 2 small fins that are on either side of the head and a small strip off the end of the tail. Next, the fish need to be skinned. Place them on a chopping board and scrape a small flap of skin off the tail with a sharp knife. Then grip this with a cloth or paper towel and pull it back towards the head, tearing it off the flesh. Turn the fish over and repeat with the second skin.

—— If they aren't going to be cooked immediately, place them in a bowl of cold water or milk, cover in clingfilm and return to the fridge. Storing in milk has the advantage that the milk proteins will caramelise when the fish is fried, adding colour and sweetness to the fish.

—— Before cooking, start to prepare the sauce. Chop a handful of flat or curly leaf parsley (or ideally a mixture), and put it in a cup with the juice of a lemon and a generous pinch of lemon zest. Another lemon, which will be used to dress the plates, needs to be peeled, de-pipped and cut into thin slices.

—— When it is time to cook the fish, dry them off with a paper towel and dredge them in flour seasoned with fine sea salt and coarse black pepper. Any flour will do, but stone-ground wheat flour is best. Dredge by putting flour on a plate and rolling both sides of the fish in it before tapping off any excess flour.

—— Prepare one frying pan per fish by heating 4 tablespoons of sunflower oil on a high heat. Sprinkle a pinch of flour in the oil; when it sizzles, the pan is ready to receive a knob of butter. This will melt fast and rise into a splattering

· · · →

foam. Gently place the fish in the pan and turn down the heat to a moderate-low temperature. Cook for 3 minutes (a little more if you have a larger fish) before turning it over carefully by sliding a fish slice under it from the tail-end. Cook the second side for 2-3 minutes, and spoon the hot oils over the cooked side regularly. A good test for the cooking of flat fish is to press your finger into the point where the back-bone meets the head. If the flesh falls away from the bone then it is cooked.

THE SAUCE:

— When ready, place the fish on a hot plate and cover with tinfoil. Discard the oily contents of one of the pans and wipe it clean with a paper towel. Melt 80g of butter in it over a high heat, swilling it around the pan so it melts faster. When the butter starts to turn brown, turn the heat down and pour in the chopped parsley, lemon juice and capers, if they are to your taste. The pan will sizzle and splutter, and after a few seconds the sauce noisette is ready to be poured over the warm fish. Serve at once.

ⁱ Serve with the thin slices of peeled lemon, some boiled new potatoes, butter-fried mushrooms, artichoke hearts, green beans, braised chard or spinach leaves.

ⁱ Whilst sole is not considered a threatened species, many stocks are being fished in unsustainable ways. Buying a fish bearing an ecolabel encourages responsible fishing that has a less detrimental impact on the sea. Beyond conscience, a second advantage of buying MSC fish is that they come from inshore fishing boats that deliver fish to the markets daily and in perfect condition. On larger boats, the sole can be poorly packed, causing their flesh to bruise, which is noticeable as brown patches in the white flesh.

ⁱ If ecolabel sole is unavailable, this recipe also lends itself to other flat fish such as dab, flounder and plaice, or farmed fish such as tilapia and claresse.

HERRING or MACKEREL
marinade

5-6 servings

1 saucepan

Hermetically sealable jar(s)
able to hold 1½ litres

90 minutes

5 herring (or 3 mackerel),
1kg cleaned (or 700g filleted)

2 medium onions

2 large carrots

500ml water

200ml white wine

50ml white vinegar

2 lemons

2 bay leaves

20 green, black
and pink peppercorns

20 coriander seeds

2 cloves

1 sprig of fresh thyme
(or ½ tsp of dried thyme)

1 sprig of fresh tarragon
(or ½ tsp of dried tarragon)

1 large sprig of parsley

1 splash of vegetable oil

Salt & pepper

— This dish requires very fresh fish, so explain to your fishmonger that they will be marinated rather than cooked, and don't accept fish that has previously been frozen. You will save yourself a lot of time and effort if you ask them to descale and fillet your fish too.

THE MARINADE:

— Finely slice 2 onions and 2 carrots, then fry them in a little vegetable oil in a saucepan until the onions are translucent. Add the juice of a lemon, the flesh of a peeled and sliced lemon, the herbs and spices and 500ml of water, 200ml of white wine and 50ml of white vinegar. Cover and boil for 10 minutes.

THE FISH:

— Rinse the fish and, over the sink or a newspaper, hold the fish belly-side up, then slice the belly open with a small sharp knife. Empty, wash and, using the handle-end of a spoon, scrape out any black residue.

— If you are preparing the herring yourself you would be well advised to cover the work surface with newspaper before descaling the fish (or even to set up a table outdoors) as this is easier than cleaning the scales off your kitchen counter, sink and walls. Hold the fish by the head and scrape the scales with a knife with a dull blade or a spoon from the tail toward the head. Apply adequate pressure for the scales to fly off and the blade to skid along the surface of the fish without breaking the skin, and keep your strokes short and quick.

— If you are preparing mackerel, there are no scales to remove, but you need to take off the clingfilm-like layer of skin. Do this by making a shallow incision along the top of the fish from head to tail and all the way round the base of the tail. Get the blade of a short sharp knife under a flap of the skin at the tail end and pull the skin off in one firm tug.

— To lift the fish fillet off the bone, use a sharp knife to make an incision behind the fin nearest to the head and cut through the flesh to the bone. Slide the blade down the back-bone and, using the palm of your free hand, push down on the fish. The flesh separates easily from the bone. Repeat this

· · · →

technique on the other side, then discard the head, tail and backbone. Trim off the fins and the bones from the abdominal cavity. Don't worry if a few bones remain. The advantage of this method of preparation is that it will turn them soft and flexible, like short hairs.

JARRING:

— Put a thick layer of cooked carrots, onions and herbs into the bottom of your sealable jar and cover with a layer of fish. Another layer of boiled vegetables follows, then another layer of fish, and so on until all the ingredients are used. Pour the warm marinade into the jar so that it is filled to the brim and then leave to cool for 10 minutes before sealing. When the jar is at room temperature it needs to go in the fridge, where it should macerate for 3 days, and be eaten within 8 days.

ⁱ The marinated fish is delicious as a light lunch or aperitif. If prepared as a lunch, serve with boiled potatoes, boiled or scrambled eggs, pickled gherkins and a beetroot salad. If it is to be served as an aperitif, cut into bite-sized pieces and present on mini toasts or oat cakes with some fromage blanc and a sprig of chervil.

ⁱ Your herring or mackerel may contain roe. These are a delicacy, fried or grilled, and spread on bread.

Mussels and chips

MUSSELS AND CHIPS IS ARGUABLY BELGIUM'S NATIONAL DISH, KNOWN as *moules-frites* in the French-speaking south and *mosselen met frietjes* by the Flemish in the north. In the past, mussels were only found on menus during the cooler months, or as an old saying goes, during the months with an 'r' in them; today, they are in restaurants almost all year round, partly due to the widespread use of refrigerated transportation. Nonetheless, many Belgians still insist that the best time to eat mussels is when the weather is cooler. If nothing else, a steaming pot of mussels is certainly inviting on a cold winter's day.

In Belgium, mussels arrive at the table in the large black pot in which they were cooked and are invariably greeted with a look of joy by whoever ordered them and one of envy by who opted for something else.

The sheer quantity of mussels can look overwhelming, but somehow they always disappear, leaving at the bottom the tasty juices in which they were cooked. Don't forget to eat these up too: it's an essential part of the culinary experience. As to what the juices might be, that all depends on how the mussels were cooked. They can be

prepared in any number of ways, from the classic *moules à la marinière,* with onions, celery, bay leaves and parsley, or *moules au vin blanc*, a similar preparation but with extra white wine, to the heavier creamier stocks or Ardennes-style with local ham. Another tip on how to eat mussels the local way is to keep the shell from the first mussel and use it as a pincer to remove the rest from their shells. You can pop them straight in your mouth or dip them in a mussel sauce that often accompanies the dish.

For a country where mussels are so popular, it's odd that these molluscs rarely come from Belgium, but far more commonly from Zeeland in the Netherlands. Production may be negligible in Belgium, but consumption certainly isn't, with Belgians eating about 40,000 tonnes of mussels a year, or in other words an average of 4kg per person per year.

CHIPS

Accompanying any pot of mussels is always a generous portion of chips, or fries. According to one version of history, it was in Belgium in the middle of the 17th century, when the land was under the rule of the Spanish, that chips were cooked for the very first time. However, there are plenty of historical sources that tell a different story and so the true origin of the chip is likely to remain a source of contention. No matter. One thing is certain: today they form a major part of the nation's food culture, with the chip pan an essential utensil in a Belgian kitchen.

The secret to a good chip is, as any Belgian will tell you, to fry them twice. The type of potato used is also key: the most common variety in Belgium is the Bintje, a floury textured potato with a fairly high starch concentration which lends itself to making the perfect crispy, golden fry.

Chips do not, of course, only accompany mussels. They are served with many a main course, be it at home, in a local brasserie or even in a top restaurant. They are also eaten by themselves as a snack, most commonly bought in a paper cone from an outdoor chip stand, the infamous *fritkot* or *friterie*. Thousands of these stands are found up and down the country, sometimes appearing at local fairs, sometimes a permanent fixture. One of the most famous is Maison Antoine in Brussels, which has been selling fries since 1948. One of the oldest is Fritkot Max in Antwerp, which dates back to 1842.

For Belgians, the sauce that comes with their chips is very important. It may simply be tomato ketchup or mayonnaise, the national favourite that accompanies more foods than you could imagine. Or it could be one of the numerous flavoured versions of mayonnaise, such as Andalouse (add a tablespoon of tomato concentrate, a tablespoon of mixed finely chopped red and green peppers and onion), Cocktail (add 2 tablespoons of tomato ketchup, 2 teaspoons of Worcerstershire sauce, 1 teaspoon of whisky or cognac, 1 pinch of cayenne pepper or 4 drops of Tabasco sauce), Gribiche (add half a finely chopped boiled egg, 1 teaspoon of finely chopped gherkin, 1 teaspoon of finely chopped shallots and 1 teaspoon of parsley) or Tartare (add 1 tablespoon of chopped capers and another of mixed finely chopped parsley, chervil and tarragon). What is certain is that there will be some kind of sauce.

Steamed
MUSSELS

2 (large) servings

1 large casserole dish

30-40 minutes

2kg mussels

1 glass to 300ml liquid
of your choice

2 large sticks of celery

1 small leek

1 large carrot

Herbs and spices
of your choice

— How best to cook mussels is an endless source of debate and experimentation. Whilst they can be bbq'ed or dressed and grilled in half-shells, the most popular method is steamed in a large saucepan or casserole dish. A wide variety of ingredients complement the flavours of mussels, so the cook has 4 enjoyable choices to make: which cooking liquid to use, which vegetables, herbs and spices to include, which other protein (if any) to serve with the mussels, and which sauce to accompany them with. The one thing that is not debated is the method of preparing the mussels for the pot.

THE MUSSELS:

— There are 5 checks that each mussel should go through to make sure that they are alive and haven't begun the rapid process of toxification that occurs when they die.

1   Discard any mussels with broken shells. Look for this as you transfer them by hand from their packet into a sink full of cold clear water.

2   Discard any mussels that float in the water.

3   Take the mussels out of the water a few at a time and transfer them to a large bowl. Feel their weight, and give any unusually heavy ones a firm tap on the edge of the sink. The worst thing that can happen to a pot of mussels is that a silt-mussel makes its way in. These are specimen that have died on the seabed and filled with black mud. A silt mussel's shell will unhinge when firmly tapped.

4   At the same time, make sure that all the mussels are closed. Any that are open enough to slide a coin into also need a tap on the side of the sink or a gentle squeeze to give them some encouragement. If they don't close, throw them away.

5   Check for cleanliness. Barnacles are no problem, but you will want to rub off any loose mud with your fingers and pinch and pull any beards, the strong threads that the mussel uses to attach itself to the seabed. Avoid the temptation to scrub mussels clean as this will give the dish an unpleasant grey colour when cooked.

. . . →

LIQUIDS:

— The first ingredient into the pot is the liquid that will produce steam. Quantities can be as small as a glass, going up to 300ml if you want to make a generous amount of sauce. Water, white wine, champagne, cider and beer are all popular, as are vegetable stock and water flavoured with a large glass of vermouth or a small glass of aniseed-flavoured alcohol. The liquid used will influence the final flavour of the dish, but it won't be dominant. An unusual but tasty liquid is crustacean bisque. It is prepared by oven-roasting crushed shrimp, crab or lobster shells with an onion and a carrot in a 200°C oven for 20 minutes, then gently boiling the residue for 2-3 hours in 2 litres of water with a tin of chopped tomatoes, a glass of brandy and ⅓ of a bottle of white wine. The liquid, which will have reduced by half, is then sieved before being used to cook the mussels.

VEGETABLES, HERBS AND SPICES:

— Accompanying the mussels into the pot should be their trusted vegetable sidekicks: a couple of sticks of celery, a small leek and a large carrot. (These need to be chopped finely, put into the pot with the cooking liquid and cooked for 5 minutes with the lid off before being joined by the mussels.) Herbs that add their distinct aromas to this dish include chervil, fresh coriander, thyme, oregano, tarragon, parsley, dill, basil and lemongrass. Complementary spices include coriander seeds, fresh ginger, mustard, pepper, saffron, star anise, chilli and curry powder. A good rule of thumb is to select a few harmonious ingredients, rather than trying to throw in all the ingredients on the spice-rack. Popular examples are the *Provençale* mix of fresh tomato, thyme, oregano, basil, garlic, lemon juice and tomato purée, the Congo mix of lemongrass, chilli, ginger and coconut milk, the *Liègeoise* mix with chervil, pepper, mustard and cream, *à la Parisienne* with garlic and cream, and Indian with curry, star anise and cream.

COOKING:

— This is pretty straightforward: after cooking the vegetables in the liquid for 5 minutes, add the mussels. Cook with the lid on for 2 minutes on the highest heat. Give the pot a big shake, or open the lid and give the mussels a good stir with a slotted spoon to bring the ones from the bottom up to the surface, then cook for 5 more minutes on a medium heat. Take a mussel out of the pot to test it: a properly cooked mussel has the texture of a fresh gummy bear, whilst an undercooked one is reminiscent of an oyster, and an overcooked one is rubbery.

··· →

ADDITIONAL PROTEIN:

—— The cook can incorporate an additional protein to the dish in order to add a deeper flavour. Popular choices are fried bacon lardons, finely chopped Ardennes ham, finely sliced chorizo sausage, shrimps, smoked salmon, finely crumbled blue cheese or grated hard cheese. These should be stirred into the pot for the last 2 minutes of the mussels' cooking time.

THE SAUCE:

—— The pot of mussels can be served to the table directly, or you can use the cooking juices to make a richer sauce. For this option, add a tablespoon of flour to a large knob of melted butter in a small saucepan and stir or whisk in the cooking juices over a high heat. When it is bubbling and thickening, add 200ml of cream, coconut milk or tomato purée mixed with milk, and whisk again, then pour the sauce over the mussels in the large pot.

SERVING:

—— The saucepan or casserole dish should be opened at the table so everyone can inhale the rising aromas when the lid is removed. Dress the table with a large empty bowl to collect the discarded shells as well as napkins with little finger-bowls because this is unquestionably finger food. Use the shell of the first mussel you eat as a pincer to pluck the rest of the mussels out of their shells.

— Accompany the steamed mussels with hunks of crunchy bread to soak up the tasty juices at the bottom of the bowl and crisp golden chips with mayonnaise. Also delicious are a tomato and cucumber tartare (peeled and diced into a small cubes then marinated in balsamic vinegar for 15 minutes) or a green tapenade (garlic blended with young spinach leaves, parsley and raisin seed oil).

— Mussels vary in colour from white to yellow to orange. There is some debate about the reason: some say it is due to a difference of gender, whilst others attribute it to varying thicknesses of shell. Either way, they are as tasty as each other.

— Leftover mussels can be deep-fried in batter. Together with their juices, they also make an excellent base for a seafood risotto.

— The price of mussels varies according to their size and age. The youngest ones, called Extras, are 1-2 years old and are 28% flesh whilst the mature ones, called Imperial and Jumbo, are more than 4 years old and are at least 45% flesh.

— Mussels are best straight out of the sea but can be stored for a week when bought in hermetically sealed plastic containers. When sold in jute bags they keep for up to 5 days. These bags are environmentally sustainable and have the advantage of shrinking when damp, which draws the mussels together, helping them stay closed and retain their freshness.

Belgian CHIPS

🍴 1 serving

🔪 1 fat fryer

🕐 30-40 minutes

250g potatoes per person
(2-3 medium potatoes)
White beef fat
(or store-bought frying oil)

— Peel and chop the potatoes lengthwise into chips of a width of about 1cm. Removing loose starch from the cut potatoes is essential and most successfully achieved by washing them twice in plenty of cold water, then drying them. This can be done with a tea towel or by putting them in a well-aerated and warm place such as an oven that has been switched on for 5 minutes. Don't fry them until they are dry to the touch because damp chips splutter and pick up more oil when cooked.

— A Belgian chip is cooked twice in white beef fat (sold under the name *blanc de boeuf* or *ossewit* in Belgium). The first dip is at 170°C for 7 minutes. A good way of checking if the fat has come up to temperature is to toss a piece of bread into it; if it turns golden brown in 45 seconds then the fat is ready. Assuming you are using a domestic fat fryer, cook the chips a handful at a time so that the temperature of the oil remains constant. When they come out of the oil the chips should be light yellow and tender. They need a good shake to remove as much oil as possible and then to cool for 10 minutes on a piece of kitchen foil or a wire rack. Make sure that they are not resting in a tepid puddle of oil.

— The second dip, at the higher temperature of 180°C, gives the chips their golden crunch. Cook a handful at a time for 2-4 minutes, until the chips float up to the surface of the oil. Serve immediately with salt. If you need to keep them warm for a few minutes until serving, don't cover them in glass or plastic as they will turn limp in their steam. Instead, do like chip shops do, and wrap them in paper (newspaper is perfect) and tear a little hole at the top to let the steam out.

ⁱ Old potatoes are preferable to new ones. The variety of potato matters too: look for Bintje, Vitelotte, Agoria, Russet Burbank, Yukon Gold, Maris Piper and Idaho.

ⁱ Store your potatoes in a wooden box or wicker basket in a dry, cool, dark place. Don't keep them in the fridge, in a plastic bag or near other vegetables (including onions).

Fresh
MAYONNAISE

🍴 250ml

🥄 1 mixing bowl

🕐 10-15 minutes

2 egg yolks

1 tsp strong mustard

200ml sunflower

(or grapeseed oil)

½ lemon

Finely ground white pepper

Fine table salt

—— There are horror stories about curdling mayonnaise, but a couple of tricks make this easy to avoid. The first is that all the ingredients should be at room temperature, so take everything out of the fridge well ahead of time. The second is to warm the mixing bowl by rinsing it with hot water, then drying it.

—— Separate 2 eggs and whisk the yolks with a teaspoon of strong mustard. If doing this by hand they need at least 2 minutes of whisking, but in a food processor on a slow setting it will take just 30 seconds.

—— It is important to add the oil to the eggs slowly, a couple of drops at a time, until the mayonnaise starts to 'take', meaning that the liquids start to transform into a thick, creamy emulsion. The oil can then be added a generous glug at a time. In a food processor this will take 1-2 minutes, but made by hand it will take at least 5 minutes and be something of a whisk workout.

—— When it is the right consistency, add pinches of fine table salt and finely ground white pepper, and the juice and pulp of half a de-pipped lemon, then whisk until these ingredients are evenly distributed. Never season until the end as it will prevent the mayonnaise from taking. If the emulsion starts to curdle as you are mixing, put a tablespoonful of very cold water in another mixing bowl and add the curdled mayonnaise a little at a time whilst beating vigorously. It should fix itself in a minute or two.

ⓘ Using whole eggs instead of egg yolks will produce a lighter, paler, less firm, but no less delicious mayonnaise.

ⓘ Store fresh mayonnaise in the fridge at all times. It is best eaten within 24 hours of being made, but does keep in a sealed jar in the fridge for a week.

ⓘ When keeping mayonnaise in the fridge, put it on a shelf at the back as keeping it in the door will expose the mayonnaise to changes in temperature each time you open the fridge.

Flemish classics: meat in pots

ONE OF THE BEST-KNOWN DISHES FROM FLANDERS, THE NORTHERN part of Belgium, is a traditional meat stew known as *stoofvlees* in Flemish and *carbonnade flamande* in French. It is a rich beef stew made with beer and onions, a hearty dish to fill you up and keep you warm on a cold winter's evening.

Flemish beef stew is often considered to be a cousin of France's beef *bourguignon*, with the French using red wine in their recipe, while the Belgians cook their meat in one of their famous brown beers. The beer that you opt for will of course subtly change the flavour of the dish [→ see the section on cooking with beer for more about the different tastes of Belgian beers, p.72].

While the basics of the recipe remain the same, there are plenty of variations from region to region, and even from family to family. Some Belgians like to add liver or kidneys to give the stew a stronger taste, while others prefer to add a slice of gingerbread covered with mustard to give a sweet spicy touch. However you cook it, there's no denying that it is wonderful winter comfort food.

Hutsepot, known as *hochepot* in French and perhaps best translated into English as hotpot, is another well-known stew, with recipes for it dating back to the 17th century. For example, several different recipes for this stew are found in *De verstandige kock* (The sensible cook) from 1667, including one called 'Spanish hotpot'. Perhaps not so surprising given that the Spanish ruled the southern Netherlands, an area that included present-day Belgium.

Today there are many variations on the basic theme too. Depending on the recipe, the dominant meat can be beef, pork, mutton or lamb while the accompanying meat parts can also be quite diverse. *Ons kookboek*, the standard cookbook found in just about every Flemish household, includes a hotpot dish from the province of Limburg that is certainly not for the faint-hearted: its ingredients include not only beef, mutton or lamb, but also 1 pig's trotter, 1 pig tail and 1 pig's ear! [→ For our hotpot recipe, see the section on beef on p.112.]

ANYTHING GOES

In truth, just about anything can go in a hotpot. And while one or two types of meat along with potatoes and vegetables is the traditional option, in the Flemish coastal town of Koksijde for example, they pride themselves on a variant that uses fish. And somewhat surprisingly perhaps, there's nothing to stop you turning this into a vegetarian dish by using a vegetable stock and a greater variety of vegetables.

Another very Flemish specialty is *potjesvlees*, cold potted meat, or to give it its literal translation 'a little pot of meat'. Its producers are based in West Flemish towns in a part of the country known as the Westhoek, the site of many First World War battlefields. The handful of butchers who make the local potted meat formed the Order of the Potted Meat, a group aimed at raising the food's profile. In 2008, the producers secured recognition from Flanders for their regional product and at the time of writing they were seeking the same from the EU.

West Flemish potted meat is usually made from three meats known locally as the 3 Ks – *kip*, *konijn* and *kalf* (chicken, rabbit and veal). But as with so many recipes, variations abound, and this dish is certainly one that has had time to evolve: the recipe was included in *Le Viandier de Taillevent*, a document most probably written for King Charles V of France by his cook, Taillevent, in the late 14th century.

FLEMISH BEEF STEW
with beer

☪ 4 servings

⚆ 1 casserole dish (ideally enamelled cast iron)

1 frying pan

⏰ Preparation: 10 minutes

Cooking: 2 hours

800g beef

1 cup flour

4 small onions

1 large knob of butter

1 splash of vegetable oil

250ml brown beer

2 tsp thyme

2 bay leaves

2 tbsp *sirop de Liège*

(or 1 tbsp redcurrant jelly and

1 tbsp honey)

Salt & pepper

OPTIONAL:

100g liver & kidney meat

1 slice bread or *pain d'épices*

(Belgian-style gingerbread)

2 tsp mustard

1 splash of cider

(or red wine vinegar)

— Roughly chop the onions and cut the beef into pieces before coating them with flour. Expect the pieces to be of an uneven shape, but aim for them to be roughly the same weight, ideally about 25g each. For 200g of meat per person, this equates to 8 pieces each.

— Fry the cubed meat in butter in a hot pan for 10 minutes. If you are cooking for a large number of people this should be done in batches so as not to crowd the pan. Once browned on all sides, remove and transfer the meat to a deep casserole dish and fry the onions in the meat juices and a little oil until golden brown. Some cooks like to add a small amount of finely chopped liver and kidneys to the onions a few minutes before they have finished cooking to heighten the flavour of the dish. Transfer to the casserole dish and deglaze the frying pan with a bottle of brown beer such as a Westmalle double, Grimbergen, Kasteelbier donker or Maredsous 10 triple. Expect the beer to froth up when it comes into contact with the hot metal. Scrape the oil and sugars off the bottom of the pan and pour them and the liquid into the casserole dish.

— Place the casserole dish over a medium heat and bring to the boil before reducing the temperature to a low simmer. Season with the thyme, bay leaves, a pinch of salt and a couple of generous twists of freshly ground black pepper. For those who like a spicy dish, add a slice of bread or *pain d'épices* coated with mustard before covering the dish with a lid and leaving to simmer for 90 minutes.

— A few minutes before serving, whilst still on a low heat, the dish needs to be sweetened with 2 tablespoons of *sirop de Liège* or its redcurrant jelly and honey replacement. It is the interplay of this sweetness and the sour taste from the beer that gives this hearty stew its character. As you taste and adjust the seasoning, you may want to accentuate the sourness of the dish with a splash of cider or red wine vinegar. Stir well.

· · · →

ⁱ Serve in large bowls accompanied with a raw chicory and mayonnaise salad, chips, boiled potatoes or *stoemp* [→ see recipe p.88] and steamed red cabbage or boiled carrots.

ⁱ Flemish stew can be kept in the fridge for 2 days and improves overnight: it will taste best the day after you prepare it.

ⁱ In common with other stews from around the world, Flemish beef stew is made with the sub-prime steaks from the forequarter of the cow, the parts that have the muscles that move the most and are most active. Butchers in different countries name the cuts differently so there can be confusion, but the names to look out for are chuck, neck, clod, blade, brisket, shoulder, shin, shank, plate, flank, boneless short-rib and cheek. Of these cuts, the cheeks are the most tender, but also the most difficult to find. In Belgium most butchers sell pre-cubed stewing meat, which is a combination of these different cuts.

ⁱ Enamelled cast iron pans are optimal for this dish because they disperse the heat evenly through their contents. If you have a lighter saucepan you will need to compensate for this by stirring the stew regularly.

Potted
MEAT

4-5 servings

1 terrine or casserole

1 large saucepan

1 small bowl

1 large bowl

Preparation: 40 minutes

Cooking: 90 minutes

Refrigeration: 12 hours

300g veal

300g rabbit

300g chicken

2 red onions

2 carrots

2½ tbsp or 5 sheets gelatine

600ml water

200ml white wine or cider

50ml vinegar (white wine
or cider)

½ lemon

1 sprig or 1 tsp thyme

1 bay leaf

4 cloves

Pepper

OPTIONAL:

2 tbsp genever or gin

1 pinch of saffron

½ tsp cardamom seeds

— The best cuts of meat for this dish are veal hock, shin or shoulder, 2 rabbit legs and half a chicken. The rabbit and chicken can be cooked on the bone.

— Peel and slice a couple of carrots into coins. Put these into a large saucepan with a bay leaf, a teaspoon or sprig of thyme, a couple of turns of pepper and, if you would like more spices, a pinch of saffron or half a teaspoon of crushed cardamom seeds. Add 600ml of water and bring to the boil, then simmer on a low heat for 10 minutes.

— Peel 2 red onions, cut them in half and stud each half with a clove. Prepare the chicken by chopping it into 3 or 4 pieces and discarding the skin and wing. Set the onions and chicken aside with the rabbit legs while you flavour the cooking stock.

— The flavouring can either be based on grapes (white wine and white wine vinegar) or apples (cider and cider vinegar). Add 200ml of the wine or cider, 50ml of vinegar and the juice of half a lemon. Add the onion, rabbit and chicken and continue to simmer on a low heat.

— The secret to this dish is to cook these meats 'long, slow and low' – with the lid on for 1.5 hours on a very low heat.

— The veal, chopped into pieces the size of your thumb, needs to cook for just 30-35 minutes, so add it when the rabbit and chicken have been cooking for an hour. Take this opportunity to give the pot a good stir.

— When the contents of the pot have finished cooking, transfer the rabbit and chicken to a plate or chopping board to be de-boned and cut into pieces of roughly the same size as the veal, and put the veal in a terrine or casserole dish.

— Dissolve the gelatine into a mug of warm stock then return it to the pot and stir in well. If you would like to give the dish a sharper edge, add a couple of tablespoons of genever or gin to the stock.

··· →

— Put the chicken and rabbit meat in the casserole dish with the veal then cover with the gelatine-rich stock. You can either pour the stock in with the herbs, onions and carrots, or through a sieve to remove these vegetables and aromatics. The former will give a jelly that is muddy in colour but has a fuller flavour, while the latter has clear jelly and a more delicate flavour.

— When the dish has cooled to room temperature, cover it with clingfilm and put in the fridge, where it will take at least 12 hours to set.

This potted meat or *potjesvlees* will keep in the fridge for up to 4 days. It is served alone as a starter or with chips as a main course and can be accompanied by some gherkins and a green leaf salad dressed in a mustard sauce.

If you serve *potjesvlees* with chips, put it in the middle of the plate and pile the chips on top: the heat from the chips will melt the jelly and release some deliciously rich aromas.

Bring out the beer

Beer is to the Belgians what wine is to the French: an intrinsic part of the national culture, with a different type of beer for just about every occasion and every taste bud. From lightly spiced wheat beers to dark Trappist brews, from the acidic Lambic to the wide variety of fruit beers, there are quite literally hundreds of different brews and flavours.

Geographically, Belgium lies within the beer belt of Europe, with a climate conducive to growing the grains and cereals needed to brew beer, contrasting with the wine regions further south and the vodka countries of the far north. Belgium has been brewing for centuries, with beer considered for a long time as a safer and cleaner option than drinking water. By the 14th century, a brewers' guild had been founded, making it one of the oldest professional associations in the world. Today, you can visit the Belgian Brewers association in a beautiful guild house on the central square of Brussels, with its basement converted into a beer museum.

A major development in the taste of beer occurred during the Middle Ages when hops were introduced, not only improving the taste but also allowing the beer to be preserved for longer. By this point in history, monks were also busy brewing beer, as well as baking bread and making cheese. And to this day, there are still monks upholding the brewing tradition with their rich, strong ales known as Trappist beers.

Belgium is home to six Trappist breweries: Chimay, Orval, Rochefort, Westmalle, Westvleteren and Achel. Most of these brews are easily found in

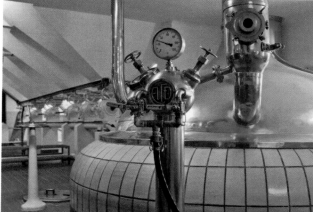

bars or supermarkets. The exception is Westvleteren, for which you have to make an appointment to visit the monks at St. Sixtus Abbey in the village of Westvleteren: a trip to the abbey is like a pilgrimage for beer lovers.

Separate from Trappist beers are the so-called Abbey beers, which bear the name of an abbey but are no longer actually brewed there. Some of these breweries have a commercial link with the abbey whose name they use; for other breweries, the connection is purely geographical. Many of these beers are similar in style to the traditional Trappists, while being more adapted to popular tastes. Some of the well-known abbey beers are Leffe, Grimbergen, Maredsous and Affligem.

Another popular beer is the white beer (*witbier* in Dutch, *blanche* in French), a light and cloudy beer flavoured with coriander and orange peel. One of the best known is Hoegaarden, the small town where the original recipe of 1445 is said to come from.

Among the most interesting Belgian beers are the Lambics. The ingredients of these acidic and naturally effervescent beers are straightforward: wheat, barley, hops and water. What makes them special is that fermentation occurs spontaneously, without the brewer introducing cultured yeasts. Instead, the beers are exposed to the air and fermented from natural yeasts found in the valley of the River Zenne/Senne, just south of Brussels, often giving these beers a sour taste.

If left to undergo a secondary fermentation, the Lambic becomes a Gueuze, a sparkling beer with a less acidic and fruitier taste sometimes referred to as Brussels Champagne. Add cherries to the mix and you get a Kriek-Lambic, a popular fruit beer. All of these Lambic beers have the European Union's Traditional Specialty Guaranteed certificate, which officially highlights their traditional character.

ONE FOR EVERY DISH

This quick tour of Belgium's major beers highlights just how many different flavours there are. The wide range of course means plenty of choice in bars, where each different beer is served in its own particular glass. However, it also means that beers can be matched with different foods and be used in interesting ways in the actual cooking of dishes.

Beers are ideal in marinades, sauces or simply as a replacement for water as the liquid in which to simmer meat. Each beer lends its own special touch: the sweetness of the fruit beers works well in salad dressings or as a sauce for duck; the spiciness of the white beers can nicely complement fish or vegetables such as asparagus, chicory or leeks; and the gentle acidity of a Gueuze can add a refreshing character to a fish soup. Whatever the dish though, be careful that you add the beer gradually or else the taste can become overpowering or bitter. And beers aren't just for savoury dishes; they can also be used when baking biscuits, cakes and breads.

When it comes to matching beer and food, a general rule of thumb is white beers work well with fish, blond beers with chicken, dark beers with dark meat and fruit beers with dessert. Cheers!

White beer poached
SALMON

4 servings

1 bain-marie
(heatproof bowl resting
on a saucepan)
1 casserole dish
2 small saucepans
2 mixing bowls

Preparation: 45 minutes
Cooking: 90 minutes

800g salmon or salmon trout
(fillets with the skin on)
1 tsp fine table salt
1 litre water
1 bottle (250ml) white beer
1 orange
1 shallot
1 large handful of coriander
1 tsp crushed coriander seeds
FOR THE SAUCE:
½ bottle (125ml) (reduced to 2
tbsp) white beer
3 eggs
100g butter
1 tsp mustard

— Boil half a bottle of white beer in a small uncovered saucepan on a medium heat for 10-15 minutes, until the volume of the liquid has reduced to about 2-3 tablespoons. This will be used in the sauce.

— Wash the fish, divide into 4 portions and place in a bowl with a heaped teaspoon of fine table salt stirred into 750ml of water and the juice of an orange. Leave the fish to brine for 15 minutes.

— Pour a bottle of white beer and 250ml of water into a casserole dish; add a sliced shallot, chopped coriander leaves, coriander seeds and the finely sliced peel of half an orange. For sweetness you can add a little tamarind, a couple of dried plums, some slices of tomato or fresh mango, or the red outer husks of a couple of rosehips. You can also add a generous turn of the pepper mill, half a teaspoon of fresh ginger, half a teaspoon of paprika and a star anise.

— Put the casserole dish containing the poaching liquid (but not the fish) in an oven heated to 170°C for 10 minutes to come up to temperature. Rinse the brine off the fish fillets then lay them in the hot liquid, skin-side down, and bake in the oven at 170°C. 7 minutes per cm of thickness of fish will turn it opaque and flaky.

THE HOLLANDAISE SAUCE:

— Melt 100g of butter in a saucepan over a low heat. When the butter has melted, turn off the heat.

— Separate the eggs. Warm the eggs yolks in a bain-marie with 2 table-spoons of beer reduction and the mustard. Beat vigorously with an electric whisk for a couple of minutes. When the mixture begins to expand and become light and frothy (like a zabaione) and forms ribbons when you lift the whisk, switch the heat off. It is crucial not to leave the pan over the steaming water for too long!

— Whisk in the liquid butter, a teaspoon at a time. The sauce will thicken and as it does you can increase the rate at which you add the butter. When it is all incorporated, the sauce should be like a rich custard.

— In a separate bowl beat the egg whites for a couple of minutes with the electric whisk until they form peaks. Then fold them into the rest of the sauce.

. . . →

— If the fish is still cooking when you fold the egg whites into the yolks, turn the heat back on under the bain-marie, but keep it very low, and stir regularly. For an extra touch of flavour, whisk 2 tablespoons of the fish's poaching liquid into the sauce just before serving.

ℹ White beer poached salmon or salmon trout should be served on warm plates with the *Hollandaise* sauce, accompanied by boiled potatoes, courgette sliced into ribbons, lightly steamed fennel and/or a watercress salad. Coriander and orange peel are used in the brewing of white beer, so a salad containing these ingredients will always pair well.

RABBIT IN BEER
with prunes

4-6 servings

1 frying pan

1 large saucepan

1 small bowl

1 small saucepan

Preparation: 30 minutes

Cooking:

1 hour 40 minutes

OPTIONAL:

Marinading: up to 24 hours

Deboning: 30 minutes

1 average-sized rabbit (± 1.3kg)

½ litre stock

100g diced smoked bacon

(or 8 slices of Ardennes ham)

2 bottles (500 ml) of Abbey,

Lambic or equally

full-flavoured dark beer

3 carrots

2 large onions

250g mushrooms

2 sticks celery

200g pitted prunes

2 tbsp *sirop de Liège* (or 1 tbsp

redcurrant jelly and honey)

8 juniper berries

2 bay leaves

1 sprig or 1 tsp thyme

1 sprig or 1 tsp rosemary

1 sprig or 1 tsp sage

1 pinch of cinnamon

— Lightly fry the bacon and onions in a little oil. At the same time, peel and chop the carrots into coins and the mushrooms into quarters. When the onions have browned, transfer the contents of the frying pan to a large saucepan. Then fry the carrots and mushrooms on a high heat for 5 minutes, before putting them in the saucepan with the bacon and onions. Chop the rabbit into 8 pieces and fry them for a couple of minutes in oil. The aim is not to cook the meat but to seal the skin.

— Put the meat in the saucepan and add the beer, juniper berries (or a splash of gin or genever if these are unavailable), ½ litre of vegetable, chicken or veal stock and the bay leaves, thyme, rosemary and sage. You can leave the ingredients to infuse and marinade for up to 24 hours in the fridge.

— Cook the rabbit and flavoured beer over a medium-low heat with the lid half on for an hour, until the meat separates easily from the bone. During this hour, soak the prunes in a small bowl of water. About 15 minutes before serving, transfer the prunes to a small pan with a generous splash of red wine or port, a pinch of cinnamon and a generous pinch of grated lemon peel, and heat through. Keep the water that the prunes have been soaking in to use later when thickening the sauce.

— You can serve the meat bones 'n all or de-bone it, in which case remove the meat from the pan and first allow it to cool. If the rabbit has been de-boned, the flesh needs to be returned to the cooking liquid and brought back up to temperature. Adjust the heat so that it bubbles gently, and add the small-diced celery and the *sirop de Liège* (or the redcurrant jelly and honey).

· · · →

1 splash of red wine or port

1 pinch of grated lemon peel

3 glugs of vegetable oil

1 tbsp cornflour

OPTIONAL:

50ml cream or milk

1 tbsp chopped parsley

THE SAUCE:

—— Mix a heaped tablespoon of cornflour with the sweet water that the prunes were re-hydrating in and stir this into the pot with a large wooden spoon. Allow the sauce to cook and thicken for 10 minutes over a medium-low heat.

—— Before serving, the dish can be made smoother by adding 50ml of cream or whole milk, and more attractive by adding a handful of chopped parsley.

ⓘ Serve the rabbit cooked in beer with the hot prunes, some *stoemp* or boiled potatoes, braised chicory and/or Brussels sprouts.

Plenty of veggies

V EGETABLES ARE THE FUTURE. WHOEVER HASN'T YET FIGURED THAT OUT is living on a different planet!" according to the Belgian chef Frank Fol, whose nickname is the Vegetables Chef because of his efforts to raise awareness about the nutritional value of vegetables and how they can contribute to a more sustainable future.

For a long time vegetables were viewed in Belgium almost exclusively as an accompaniment to meat dishes, forever playing the supporting rather than the main role. The 21st century, however, has seen a gradual shift in behaviour, with more vegetarian dishes appearing on menus, and the Belgian city of Ghent becoming the first in the world to go vegetarian once a week. Ghent's 'Veggie Thursday' concept has since taken off in other cities in Belgium and around the globe.

In Belgium, as in other countries, people are increasingly aware of their health, the environment and the importance of sustainable food production. As a result, greater emphasis is being put on eating local seasonal produce. Not only has this led to a higher profile for vegetables in general, it has also resulted in a rediscovery of some of the 'forgotten' vegetables such as chard, celeriac, beetroot and kohlrabi.

With its mild and humid climate and fertile soil, Belgium's geography is ideal for growing a wide range of vegetables. Two of the most popular are chicory and asparagus [→ covered in detail in a separate chapter along with hop shoots, see p.90]. For many people though, the vegetable most closely associated with Belgium is the Brussels sprout,

which grows in clusters on long vertical stalks and has been cultivated in the area since at least the 17th century when it helped feed a rapidly rising population.

Many of the staple vegetables found in Belgium's fields, ranging from cauliflowers, cabbages and celery to leeks, carrots and beans, have been around much longer. They were even mentioned in Charlemagne's *Capitulare de Villis*, an 8th century text that includes a list of vegetables, fruits, plants, trees and herbs grown in Medieval gardens.

Over the centuries, many other vegetables such as spinach, cucumber and aubergines have found their way to Belgium as a result of voyages of discovery, military campaigns and trade through Belgium's ports. As to what was available by the 16th century, we have a reliable source in the books of Belgian botanists, notably Rembert Dodoens, that describe in detail the vegetables and herbs of the time including hop shoots and the herb tansy.

FROM THE FIELD TO THE TABLE

Today, one of Belgium's major production centres for vegetables is Sint-Katelijne-Waver, near Mechelen (halfway between Brussels and Antwerp). This is also where Europe's largest co-operative auction, the Auction of Mechelen, can be found. With some 2,000 market gardeners as its member shareholders, the Auction of Mechelen aims to sell its members' produce under the best conditions. The day before the auction, the growers bring their vegetables for inspection and classification, with top-quality products being awarded the Flandria label. The next day the produce is sold at auction and delivered in refrigerated lorries to shops and supermarkets.

So what are some of the traditional ways of cooking all these vegetables in Belgium? There's no denying that the Belgians love cooking with butter and cheese, and this is no exception when it comes to vegetables: beans or carrots cooked in butter, and cauliflower or potatoes au gratin are all popular side dishes. Vegetable soups are standard winter fare, with some places renowned for their local specialty such as Aalst for its onion soup, Mechelen for its cauliflower soup and the Ardennes for its milk soup made from leeks, potatoes, onions, and of course milk. Vegetables whose names reflect their country of origin include *Roi des Belges* (King of the Belgians) green beans and *Glorie van Mechelen* (Glory of Mechelen) tomatoes.

No matter which vegetables you prefer, you can always make one typical Belgian dish: *stoemp*, which is essentially mashed potatoes combined with any number of possible vegetables. A common choice is green cabbage *stoemp*, which is mashed potato – not too creamy, not too hard – with small pieces of cabbage in it. Other popular vegetables to use are carrots, broccoli and sprouts, but there are no rules as to what can or cannot be included. *Stoemp* is found on virtually all Belgian menus, usually as a side dish to accompany sausages: vegetables may well be taking on an increasingly important role, but their popularity as a side dish remains strong.

Vegetable
PICKLES

1 litre

1 large bowl

2 or 4 sealable glass jars

Preparation: 40 minutes

Marinading: 2 weeks

2 fresh gherkins or 1 cucumber

½ cauliflower

4 celery stalks

4 carrots

1 fennel

125g mini corn cobs

100g fresh cocktail onions

Sea salt

FOR THE SAUCE:

1 litre distilled malt vinegar

6 tbsp mild mustard

3 tbsp cane sugar

5 tbsp plain flour

1 tbsp turmeric

Juice of ½ lemon

— Wash the vegetables and cut them all into small chunks. Place all the vegetables in a large bowl and generously sprinkle with sea salt. The vegetables now need to be left in the fridge for at least 24 hours; this will allow the salt to draw the excess moisture out of the vegetables in order to preserve their flavour and texture.

— Once the vegetables are ready, take them out of the fridge, rinse thoroughly and drain. For the sauce, simply whisk all the ingredients together.

— Rinse your glass jars with boiling water to sterilise them and then fill with the vegetables, cover with the sauce and seal.

— Leave the pickles in a cool, dark place for at least 2 weeks before opening them.

Once open the vegetable pickles will last for about a week, so it's best to divide them between several small jars rather than put them all in one big jar. The volumes given in this recipe can be split into 2 jars of ½ litre or 4 jars of ¼ litre. Unopened, the vegetable pickles will last at least 2 months.

Vegetable STOEMP

🍴 4 servings

🔪 1 large saucepan

1 potato masher

🕐 45 minutes

500-600g potatoes

400-500g vegetables

1 large onion

1 garlic clove

large knob of butter

550ml vegetable or chicken
stock

Salt & pepper

80ml milk (if preparing green
stoemp)

OPTIONAL:

2 egg yolks

100ml cream

50g butter

100g cheese

— This popular dish is a mixture of potato and a seasonal vegetable and comes in 3 colours: white, yellow and green. White is made from potato mixed with celeriac, parsnip, swede or salsify; yellow is made with carrot or pumpkin; and green contains broccoli, leeks, cabbage, courgette, peas, spinach or sprouts. Stoemp is made in proportions of either 60:40 if using potato and green vegetables or 50:50 if using potato and another root vegetable. As with most Belgian dishes, stoemp can be enriched with cheese, butter and cream.

— Peel and cut the floury potatoes into 1cm cubes. At the same time, fry a large, coarsely chopped onion in a knob of butter in a large saucepan until translucent. Add the diced potato, 550ml of stock, a sliced clove of garlic, and some salt and pepper. If you are making white or yellow stoemp, the vegetables should go into the pot at the same time as the potato. However, as green stoemp is made from more fragile watery vegetables, these don't go into the pot until 15 minutes after the potatoes.

— Cover and cook on a medium-low heat for 25 minutes without stirring.

— When cooked, the contents of the pot need to be *stoemped*. In order to get the consistency you want – somewhere between a stew and a smooth mash – fork-squash the boiled cubes of potato and chopped vegetables, or pass them through a food-mill with large holes, or squash just once with a potato masher. Then stir with a wooden spoon to help the potatoes absorb the remaining cooking liquid. Green stoemp made from watery vegetables (broccoli, cabbage, courgette and peas in particular) benefits from having the stock removed after cooking and replacing with 80ml of milk before *stoemping*.

— For a richer stoemp, stir in 2 egg yolks, 100ml of cream, 50g of butter or 100g of strong semi-hard cheese, such as Chimay or Herve.

🍴 If you are preparing a carrot stoemp from a bunch of fresh young carrots, wash the green leaves, then chop finely and stir into the stoemp to give it a fresher flavour and colour.

Under-
ground
trio

Who would have thought there were so many uses for chicory, a vegetable that many people outside Belgium would have trouble identifying? Not only can its root be used as a coffee substitute and its white leaves in salads and warm dishes, but the Belgians have also experimented with a chicory jam, a chicory liqueur and even a chicory beer.

The cultivation of chicory (also known as *chicon*, *witloof* and Belgian endives) had its origins in the Brussels district of Schaerbeek in the mid-19th century. It was Franciscus Bresiers, then head gardener of the Botanical Gardens (located in Schaerbeek), who is credited with having developed the tightly packed cone of white chicory leaves that we know today.

Around 1870, growing chicory was mainly limited to Schaerbeek and the neighbouring district of Evere, but in the decades that followed it expanded further afield. Today, the traditional chicory is grown in a geographical area that takes in much of Brussels and its surroundings; it is called Brussels *grondwitloof* (Brussels ground chicory), is an EU-protected product and can be identified by a special logo that indicates the vegetable was grown in soil. The more commonly sold chicory in Belgium these days, however, is a hydroponic variety.

Belgians are the biggest consumers of chicory worldwide, eating on average 6.5kg per year, according to the Flemish women farmers' association KVLV. They're not the only ones who love the vegetable though. The late Greek shipping tycoon Aristotle Onassis is said to have come to Belgium by private plane in order to stock up on chicory at auction and much of the chicory sold in the United States comes from Belgium.

So what is it that makes the vegetable that little bit different? One characteristic is its bitterness, a taste rarely found in other vegetables. The greener the chicory tip, the more bitter the taste. If you want to offset some of that bitterness when eating them raw, a good accompaniment is orange or grapefruit. Or enjoy them cooked as *chicons au gratin*, a typical dish found on the menu of just about every Belgian brasserie. [→ see recipe p.94]

The nutritional value of chicory shouldn't be overlooked either. It has a high mineral content and is a good source of vitamin C, iron and calcium. And if you want to boost the health factor, you could always go on the chicory walk or take the chicory cycling route in Kampenhout, a Belgian town that has built up its profile around the vegetable, even boasting a chicory museum with a neighbouring restaurant (the Veilinghof) that specialises in chicory dishes.

EXPENSIVE TASTE

This part of the country, and in particular nearby Mechelen, is very well known for its white asparagus too. White asparagus, which owes its colour to the fact it is grown underground and so not exposed to photosynthesis, is larger, sweeter and more tender than its green counterpart.

The arrival of white asparagus in the shops in Belgium is considered a real highlight of the culinary calendar. Only available between April and early June, the season is short and, as such, the vegetable commands a fairly high price.

Not as high a price as hop shoots, however. Hop shoots are considered to be the most expensive vegetable in the world, with the season's first harvest sold at auction for as much as 999 euro per kg, according to the Flemish tourist board. Their price has earned them the nickname of 'white gold', quite a change from times gone by when the shoots were considered food for the peasants. To prepare the shoots, which are available from March until mid-April, simply give them a gentle clean and steam lightly.

Hop shoots used to grow across much of the country, but today it is the town of Poperinge that is known as the vegetable's mecca. Poperinge hosts an annual Hop Shoots Festival, during which top restaurants add the vegetable to their upmarket menus. Guided tours through hop fields are also possible and if your budget doesn't stretch to the hop shoot dishes, there's always the beer to taste. Poperinge is also home to the Hop Museum, where you can learn about the history and culture of this precious shoot. After all, it does have a tradition that goes back to the Middle Ages.

CHICORY
with ham & cheese

4-6 servings

1 ovenproof dish (or 2 smaller gratin dishes)
1 frying pan
2 small pans

Preparation: 40 minutes
Cooking: 40 minutes

4 chicory
4 wet-cured ham slices
1 small onion
100g grated cheese
400ml milk
2 tbsp plain flour
2 tbsp butter
1 lemon
1 bay leaf
1 sprig or 1 tsp thyme
1 tsp peppercorns
½ tsp grated nutmeg
Salt & pepper
OPTIONAL:
1 tsp brown sugar
Worcestershire sauce

— Wash and dry the chicory, remove any damaged leaves and, using a small sharp knife, scoop out the core from the base of each head of chicory. Some of the core needs to remain so that the chicory doesn't fall apart.

— Fry the whole chicory in a tablespoon of butter in a covered pan over a medium heat for 15 minutes. Turn regularly so that all sides are cooked. If you want to offset some of the vegetable's bitter taste, add a teaspoon of sugar during the last 5 minutes of cooking. Turn off the heat and squeeze the juice of a lemon over the chicory. Set aside until they are cool enough to hold.

— Bring the milk to the boil in a pan with a bay leaf, the thyme, peppercorns and a small roughly chopped onion. Keep an eye on the pan as milk tends to boil over quickly. Once boiled, simmer for 5 minutes. Turn the oven to 180°C.

— In another pan, melt 2 tablespoons of butter. Remove from the heat and add 2 tablespoons of flour. Mix it in and then pour in about a third of the boiled milk through a sieve (to remove the onion, peppercorns and herbs). Whisk vigorously before adding the rest of the milk and mixing again. Bring to the boil and allow to bubble gently for 4-5 minutes. Add half a teaspoon of ground nutmeg, and some salt and pepper.

— Wrap each chicory in a slice of pink wet-cured ham and place them in a single layer in an ovenproof dish or in individual gratin dishes. Pour the sauce over the chicory and top with grated cheese. Gruyere, Emmental, mature Cheddar, Oude Brugge or an abbey cheese complement the bitter flavour of chicory well. A few drops of Worcestershire sauce on the cheese will make the cheese go a darker richer brown. In that case, don't flavour the sauce with extra salt and pepper.

— Place in the middle of a pre-heated oven at 180°C for 40 minutes. If the cheese has not browned, finish it off under the grill for 5-10 minutes.

Flemish-style ASPARAGUS

2 servings
Kitchen string
2 saucepans
1 small bowl
1 heatproof bowl
30 minutes

8-10 white asparagus spears
3 hard boiled eggs
100g butter
1 ½ tsp salt per litre of water
1 handful of parsley
1 splash of vinegar

— Peel the stems of the asparagus from 3cm below the tip to 3cm from the base. Snap the base off by holding it with one hand and the middle of the spear with the other, and bend: the asparagus will snap at the place where tender flesh meets woodier fibres.

— Salt the water with 1½ teaspoons of salt per litre of water. Gently boil the asparagus for 5-10 minutes, depending on their thickness and freshness. Aim to keep the delicate tips above the boiling water, where they will cook more slowly in the rising steam. A tall, thin saucepan facilitates this, as does an upturned heatproof bowl placed in a wider saucepan. Divide the asparagus into 2 equal-sized bunches and tie them together with kitchen string. Lean the bunches against each other to prevent them from cooking horizontally.

— The asparagus are ready when the tip of a knife can pierce a stem without effort. Remove with pincers or a slotted spoon and tap off any excess water.

A LA FLAMANDE SAUCE:

— Whilst *Hollandaise* sauce [→ see p.76] is a fine complement, the most popular sauce is *à la Flamande*: 3 eggs that are boiled for 10 minutes in water with a splash of vinegar, then peeled, mashed with a fork and mixed into 100g of melted butter and a handful of finely chopped parsley.

ℹ Asparagus should be eaten as soon after harvesting as possible. The best asparagus are available from early April to early June. Look for ones with fat, firm, undamaged stems and pearly-white tips. The spears should make a squeaking noise when rubbed together, and a moistness should appear on the base when squeezed between thumb and forefinger.

ℹ Stored in a cool, damp and dark place, asparagus will keep for 2-3 days after purchase. Wrap the stems in a damp cloth and put them in the vegetable box of a fridge. Ensure that the tips are kept dry and not wrapped in the damp cloth.

ℹ Asparagus is a versatile ingredient, pairing best with salty and sulphurous accompaniments. Air-dried Ardennes ham cut paper-thin is popular, as is seafood such as crab, shrimps and lobster, smoked salmon, trout, turbot and caviar. Morel and shiitake mushrooms, black truffles and globe artichoke will also set off the asparagus' flavours, while parmesan and mature cheddar have a similar salty-butteriness to the *à la Flamande* sauce.

Pork in all its forms

NOTHING GOES TO WASTE WHEN A PIG IS SLAUGHTERED IN BELGIUM: not only are the different cuts of meat consumed, but also the internal organs and even the pig's blood, used to make Belgians' beloved blood sausages. There's even a French expression for this: *'tout est bon dans le cochon'*, which literally means that everything in a pig is edible and is also used figuratively to say that every part of something can be put to good use.

Pork, in all its different forms, is the meat that Belgians consume the most. In fact pork accounts for almost half of the country's annual meat consumption. Belgium is also a big pork exporter, with the meat being Flanders' most important export product in the agricultural and horticultural sector.

For the meat that stays in Belgium, the nation has countless ways of preparing it. A popular choice on Belgian menus is a knuckle of ham: just make sure you have a big appetite, as it is quite literally a huge chunk of meat on the bone. In some parts of the country, roasted pork belly (known as *hâte levée* in Wallonia) is another common find on menus. In bars you can often order cold jellied pork meat, which is typically made from a pig's head and sometimes from its ears and tail too; known as *kip-kap*, *geperste kop* or *tête pressée*, depending on the exact preparation, it is served with mustard as a snack to accompany beer. In Belgian homes, warm stews are regular winter fare. And that's without mentioning all the different pâtés, terrines and sausages.

Among the range of sausages enjoyed in Belgium, high on the list are blood sausages, known as *boudins* in French and *pensen* in Flemish. The nearest equivalent in the English-speaking world is black pudding. In Belgium, these pork sausages come in two colours, black and white, although pig's blood is only actually used in the black ones. As well as being served in restaurants and sold at butchers, the sausages are also a popular snack at outdoor festivals and fairs.

TRADITION

In Brussels, the local blood sausage is called *Bloempanch*. About 15 centimetres in diameter, the Bloempanch is much bigger than its regional counterparts and is eaten in slices. The capital city's pride in this local specialty is reflected in Den Bloempanchgang, a street in the Marolles district named after the sausage, and the Order of the Bloempanch, a group seeking to highlight the product's cultural heritage and whose honorary members include the Michelin-starred Belgian chef Pierre Wynants.

Other towns around the country have their pork specialties too. For example in Mons you'll find pork chops with *berdouille* sauce, the name for which comes from the local word for mud and which is made with mustard, white wine, vinegar, shallots and pickled gherkins. In Liège, pigs' kidneys are a specialty. And the Ardennes region, the wooded area in the south, is renowned for its lightly smoked roast pork.

Two areas of Belgium have even gained EU protection for their pork products: the Gaume region for its *pâté Gaumais*, and the Belgian province of Luxembourg (as well as certain districts bordering on the provinces of Liège and Namur) for the *jambon d'Ardenne* ham.

Pâté Gaumais is a baked pie filled with chunks of quality pork marinated according to a traditional recipe that includes wine, vinegar, onions, bay leaves and juniper berries. The round pie, with a diameter of at least 15 centimetres and weighing at least 200 grams, is made in an area bound to the north by the Ardennes forest, the east by the district of Arlon and the west and south by France. The locals are such lovers of the food that every year they organize a competition, held in Virton, to find the person who can eat the most *pâté Gaumais* in 20 minutes!

As for *jambon d'Ardenne*, this ham must be salted, matured and smoked in the Ardennes since it is the region's microclimate, including the temperature and the humidity, that gives the ham its characteristics. The dried ham, which is eaten as part of a platter of cold meats, on a slice of bread or in warm dishes such as soups, is part of a long tradition in the Ardennes. We know from menus, manuscripts and books that the ham has been served to travellers and eaten at festivities in the area for centuries.

The importance of the pig and its association with feasting is reflected in Brueghel's 16th century painting *The Battle of Carnival and Lent*, where Carnival is depicted as a rotund man straddling a barrel of beer and holding a skewer with a pig's head and sausages. Some 400 years on and the pork tradition is still very much alive.

Gaume
MEAT PIE

🍴 1 pie (4 servings)

🔪 1 large Tupperware

1 mixing bowl

1 small bowl

🕐 Preparation: 1 ¾ hours

Marinading:

24-48 hours

Cooking: 50 minutes

800g pork chops or fillet

FOR THE MARINADE:

1 glass white or red wine

5 tbsp wine or cider vinegar

1 tbsp olive oil

3 shallots

2 garlic cloves

1 tsp thyme

3 bay leaves

3 cloves

1 handful of parsley

Salt & pepper

FOR THE PASTRY:

500g plain flour

20g fresh yeast

150g butter

200ml milk

3 eggs

1 pinch of salt

— In a Tupperware, mix together the ingredients of the marinade. Trim any bones and fat off the pork, then cut the meat into 2cm wide cubes and mix into the marinade. Store the Tupperware in the fridge for 24-48 hours, stirring morning and evening. The pork will become more flavoursome and tender the longer it marinades.

— On the day you cook the pie, prepare the pastry by mixing the warm milk with the crumbled fresh yeast and a pinch of salt. Let it rest for 15 minutes while you sift 500g of plain flour into a mixing bowl. Beat 2 of the 3 eggs in a small bowl, add the yeasty milk, then pour the liquid into a well in the middle of the flour. Add the soft butter, then bring the dough together. Cover it with a damp tea towel and leave it in a warm place for 60 minutes to rest.

— Switch the oven to 200°C, then knead the dough on a floured work surface. Cut off about a fifth of the dough (this will be used later) and set aside. Divide the remaining dough into a smaller piece (⅓ of the dough) that will form the base and a larger piece (⅔ of the dough) that will make the lid. Roll out the 2 layers so that the smaller base has a diameter of about 25cm and the larger lid is 3cm wider on each side.

— Put the base section on a greased baking tray. Discard the marinade and the onions and place the meat on the pastry, leaving a 3cm border around the edges. Season, then lay the lid piece over the top and seal the 2 layers of dough by pushing them together firmly with your thumbs.

— Cut the ball of the remaining dough into 6 pieces and roll each of these out to the length of your forearm. Make 2 braids, each with 3 strands, and rest them round the circumference of the pie, pushing down gently so that they attach to the pie. Separate the third egg, whisk the yolk with a fork, then brush it over the top of the pie and the braid.

— Make 3 holes the diameter of a pencil in the top of the pie, to let the steam out. Cook in the centre of an oven for 50 minutes at 200°C.

— Gaume meat pie can be eaten hot or cold.

Blood SAUSAGE

2 servings

1 frying pan

1 small bowl

1 baking / roasting tin
(optional)

30 minutes

300g blood sausage
(*boudin noir/zwarte pens*)

1 cooking apple

1 large shallot

50g butter

1 tsp brown sugar (or honey)

1 pinch of ground nutmeg

1 pinch of ground cinnamon

OPTIONAL:

1 handful of redcurrants
(or blackberries)

100ml cider or sherry vinegar

— Soften and brown a sliced shallot in butter for 10 minutes on a medium heat. Whilst this is cooking, peel and de-core a sour cooking apple and cut it into 8 pieces. Once this is cooked, remove and set aside. Next, fry the apple in a knob of butter with a teaspoon of brown sugar or honey to help it caramelise. Add pinches of ground cinnamon and nutmeg and cook on a medium heat for 7-8 minutes. If you have some fresh or frozen redcurrants or blackberries, these can be heated through in the pan when the apple has caramelized.

— The blood sausage can either be baked in the oven at 180°C for 15 minutes or fried in a little butter on a medium heat for 4-8 minutes. A simple complementary sauce can be made by deglazing the pan with a splash of cider or sherry vinegar and a knob of butter.

ⓘ There are as many recipes for *boudin noir/zwarte pens* as there are butchers making it. Each uses different proportions and combinations of blood and blood-rich meat, as well as bread, egg, butter, suet, onions, leeks, cabbage, pine nuts, apple, raisins, wine, nutmeg, cloves, ginger, nutmeg, chilli powder, rosemary, thyme, hyssop and marjoram. All blood sausages are cooked during their production and so can be eaten hot, as explained in this recipe, or cold (a popular aperitif).

ⓘ Blood sausage accompanied by the apple and berries can be served with a baked potato, *stoemp* or dark rye bread, and any number of the following: onion marmalade, pungent Tierenteyn or Bister mustard, scrambled egg, sautéed fennel, Brussels sprouts, braised red cabbage, redcurrant jelly or a chicory salad.

About cows and steaks

THE STORY OF BEEF IN BELGIUM IS DOMINATED BY THAT OF THE BELGIAN Blue, a breed of cattle that has been developed over more than a century to create what is today considered a muscular beauty by its proponents and a monster by its critics.

The name Belgian Blue (*Blanc Bleu Belge* in French and *Belgisch Witblauw* in Flemish) refers to one of the breed's typical colourings: blue and white. The name was adopted in 1973 following a significant development in the breeding of these Belgian cows. Until the middle of the 20th century, the aim had been to create a dual-purpose breed that could provide milk and beef; during the 1960s, however, the emphasis moved towards raising an animal just for its meat. The result was an extremely muscular breed that provides lean cuts.

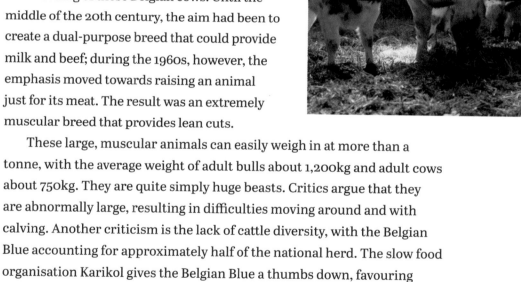

These large, muscular animals can easily weigh in at more than a tonne, with the average weight of adult bulls about 1,200kg and adult cows about 750kg. They are quite simply huge beasts. Critics argue that they are abnormally large, resulting in difficulties moving around and with calving. Another criticism is the lack of cattle diversity, with the Belgian Blue accounting for approximately half of the national herd. The slow food organisation Karikol gives the Belgian Blue a thumbs down, favouring instead the Limousine, Blonde d'Aquitaine, Blanc bleu mixte and Charolais breeds. Other smaller-scale breeds in Belgium include the Rootbont from West Flanders and the Pie Rouge in the East of the country.

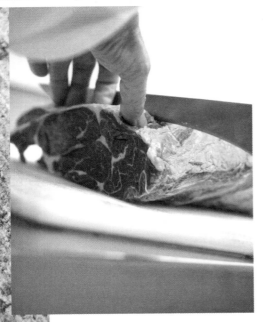

Whatever type of beef is used, Belgians have many ways of cooking this meat. Steak, accompanied with the nation's favourite side dish of chips, is one of the most popular [→ for how to prepare a steak, see p.110]. A typical Belgian menu won't just have one type of steak on offer but several, including a steak fillet, a rib steak and an *onglet* cut (also known in English as a skirt steak). As for how the meat is cooked, it's anywhere between very rare and medium, with well-done being mainly reserved for (British) tourists.

Interestingly, some of the words used for steak are taken from the English language, with *steak*, *bifteck* and *biefstuk* commonly used. Linguistic borrowings are also found in reference to roast beef, which is often closely associated with England but also eaten in Belgium where it is called *rosbif* or *rosbief*.

A WIDE VARIETY

Beef is also enjoyed raw in Belgium. Finely chopped high-quality meat, known as *steak tartare* or *filet américain*, is on the menu both in top restaurants and your average brasserie. Served on lightly toasted bread, it is called 'cannibal toast'.

As far as salted and smoked beef is concerned, the *filet d'Anvers* (literally the Antwerp fillet) is probably the best known, not least because it is a recognised regional product in Flanders.

As with other meats, the Belgians are not shy about eating just about any part of the animal. Veal kidneys are considered a specialty in Liège, while Brussels is known for *choesels*, an old-fashioned dish made with the pancreas according to some and testicles according to others. The liver and tail of the cattle are other ingredients used to beef up this dish, with everything being left to cook in a sauce of herbs and either Lambic beer or Madeira fortified wine.

On the subject of tradition, a text about cattle would not be complete without a reference to the winter fair and livestock market in Sint-Lievens-Houtem. On November 11 and 12 every year, the Flemish village is transformed by the event, which is recognised by UNESCO as an example of Intangible Cultural Heritage of Humanity. For two days, farmers, dealers and thousands of visitors gather for the open-air market where transactions take place using the old technique of a clap of the hands indicating a sale. Tradition is alive and kicking.

Grilled STEAK

 1 serving

1 frying pan

20 minutes

150-200g steak

2 tbsp oil

Salt & pepper

FOR THE SIMPLE SAUCE:

1 large knob of butter

1 small handful of parsley

FOR THE RICH SAUCE:

50ml cognac

200ml beef or chicken stock

200ml cream

1 chopped and fried shallot

1 tsp green peppercorns

—— Ask the butcher for a tender sirloin, fillet or rib-eye that is 2-3cm thick and dark plum in colour. Remove it from the fridge and leave at room temperature covered with a cloth for at least an hour, and ideally half a day, before cooking. Make sure you have all your accompaniments pre-prepared as the steak will cook quickly.

—— Season the steak with salt but not pepper as it would burn in the very hot pan that the steak needs to cook well. Cover the meat in a layer of olive oil on both sides and place in the pan presentation side down (expect it to sizzle and splutter). Turn the steak once, or once a minute, or every 15 seconds; whichever you choose, cooking the steak should have your full attention.

—— Test if the steak is ready by pushing it with 2 fingers; if it feels like pushing into the softest part of the palm of your hand, between the thumb and index finger, then the steak is rare. If it feels like pushing into the ball of the thumb then it is medium and if it feels like pushing into the inside of the wrist then it is well done. Don't cut into the steak to see how it is cooking as this will make the juices run out of the meat. While turning the steaks, use tongs to pick them up and press them down on their fatty edge to force out the juices.

—— When ready, take the steak out of the pan, season with pepper and rest it for 5 minutes on a very hot plate. If you are making the cream sauce, the plated steaks can be popped under the grill at a low temperature for a few extra minutes.

A SIMPLE SAUCE:

—— Turn down the heat, add 150ml of water to the frying pan and deglaze the pan by scraping up the sediment. Add a large knob of butter and when it has melted, a handful of chopped parsley.

A RICH SAUCE:

—— Turn down the heat, add a shot of cognac (watch out for flames!) and deglaze with stock, to which you add the cream, a teaspoon of fresh green peppercorns and a fried shallot, before reducing the sauce to half its volume over a high heat.

Beef
HUTSEPOT

🍴 4-6 servings

🔪 1 large saucepan

🕐 Preparation: 20 minutes
Cooking: 1½-2 hours

1½ litres stock or water

500g stewing beef

1 beef marrowbone

300g mutton or lamb

200g smoked sausage

(or pork belly)

4 small onions

4 garlic cloves

4 large or 8 small potatoes

4 large carrots

2 parsnips

2 small turnips

¼ celeriac

1 leek

½ savoy cabbage

(or 15-20 Brussels sprouts)

1 tsp nutmeg

2 bay leaves

1 tsp thyme

½ tsp marjoram

2 cloves

4 juniper berries

6 black peppercorns

1 tsp powdered ginger

Salt & pepper

— Pour 1½ litres of stock or water into a large saucepan and add a beef marrowbone, a sliced smoked sausage or pieces of smoked pork belly, roughly chopped onions, peeled cloves of garlic, and the bay leaves, thyme, marjoram, cloves, juniper berries, black peppercorns and powdered ginger. Put on a high heat and bring to the boil.

— Trim any fat off the stewing beef and mutton/lamb and chop into thumb-sized pieces. When the cooking liquids start to boil, turn the heat down to low and add the meat to the pan. Cover and set a timer for 60 minutes.

— Meanwhile, peel and cube the potatoes and carrots and when the timer goes off, put them in the pan. Turn the heat up a little bit.

— Wash and chop the celeriac, leek, parsnips and turnips. These softer vegetables go into the pot 15 minutes after the hard ones. Add the shredded savoy cabbage or Brussels sprouts 15 minutes after the soft vegetables. (If your pot isn't large enough to accommodate all this food, the green vegetables can also be steamed or boiled in a separate pan for 10-15 minutes.)

— Add the nutmeg 5 minutes before serving and adjust the seasoning if necessary. If you have used smoked sausage in the dish then you probably don't need to add any extra salt.

— Serve hutsepot in heated bowls with a ladleful of the cooking stock. Mustard and horseradish sauce go well with the dish.

🛈 The strained cooking stock from this dish can be served as a soup starter the following day.

🛈 As with most recipes calling for juniper berries, when these are unavailable, they can be replaced with a small splash of similar tasting gin or genever.

There's always minced meat

To GET AN IDEA OF BELGIANS' RELATIONSHIP WITH MINCED MEAT, LOOK no further than the window of any Belgian butcher. There you will find the widest range of preparations that you've possibly ever seen. Alongside the minced pork, beef and veal, you'll find combinations such as minced beef and pork or pork and veal, and a little further along you'll see Belgians' beloved *filet américain*, minced meat that is eaten raw. Then there are the meatballs, the burgers, meatloaf, blind finches... the list seems endless.

Blind finches, which go by the same name in Flemish (*blinde vinken*) and are known in French as headless birds (*oiseaux sans têtes*), are so-called because of their shape, not what they're made of. They are in fact put together from a minced meat preparation moulded into a shape that more or less resembles the body of a small bird and then wrapped in a thin slice of beef. They can be made at home [→ the full recipe is provided on p.118] or bought from the butcher ready to pop straight in the oven.

Meatballs sound straightforward enough. Not in Belgium. Here they come in all sorts of shapes and sizes and are served with different sauces and accompaniments depending on when they're eaten. Small meatballs, about the size of a marble, are added to tomato soup to produce a richer flavour. Then there are medium-sized ones that can be served with a tomato or gravy sauce [→ see the recipe on p.120 for the famous Liège-style meatballs]. And then there are larger meatballs, commonly sliced and eaten as a sandwich filling.

Or fill the meatball with a boiled egg and you have the Flemish favourite *vogelnestjes*, which literally means 'little bird's nests'.

Another variation that Belgians enjoy is to bake the meatball mixture like a loaf and then serve it in slices, either hot or cold. In Flanders, people call this *frikadellenkoek*. There are also *fricadelles* or *frikadellen*, meatballs that are often served with sour cherries: the Flemish cooking Bible *Ons kookboek* recommends this dish as a brunch, although traditionally it is a combination that is enjoyed at outdoor fairs.

In Namur, the capital of Wallonia, one local specialty is the *avisance*. Made from minced meat wrapped in pastry, it is a popular snack during the town's annual *Fêtes de Wallonie* (Wallonia festival). The food's origin is said to lie with the people of Namur, who on their pilgrimages in days gone by would take pancakes stuffed with meat leftovers to keep up their strength. The pilgrims said they were being resourceful, or in French *avisaient*, hence the name.

RAW FACTS

All the above are, of course, ways that Belgians *cook* minced meat. This is a nation, however, that also has a particularly soft spot for eating raw minced beef, or *filet américain* as it is known here. The dish is said to have been introduced by the Belgian Joseph Niels about a century ago. Having worked in the Savoy Hotel in London, Niels returned home in the 1920s and opened the Canterbury, a hotel restaurant on Boulevard Emile Jacqmain in central Brussels, and it is there that he created his *filet américain*.

While there are variations on what is included in *filet américain*, one basic recipe is raw minced beef (it is essential that the meat is very fresh and of high quality), mixed with egg yolk, chopped gherkins, shallots, capers, Tabasco sauce and seasoning. For some, it is the addition of mayonnaise and piccalilli that really makes the difference.

Filet américain is a dish that is found at both extremes of the dining experience. On the one hand it is served in pricey restaurants, where it is usually accompanied with chips. Yet it is also a very popular sandwich filling, and rare is the local sandwich bar or delicatessen that doesn't offer some variant of an *américain*. The prize for the best-named dish, however, has to go to 'cannibal toast', which is the raw minced beef mixture on lightly toasted bread.

Blind
FINCHES

- 4 servings
- 70-80cm kitchen string
- 1 mixing bowl
- 1 frying pan
- 1 large saucepan
- Tinfoil
- Preparation: 30 minutes
  Cooking: 30 minutes

4 thin beef or veal steaks
200g minced pork/veal
1 egg
2 slices of bread
100ml milk
500ml meat or vegetable stock
1 knob of butter
1 splash oil
3 shallots
1 garlic clove
4 carrots
250g mushrooms
1 tbsp flour
1 tsp thyme
1 tsp sage
1 bay leaf
1 lemon
1 handful of parsley
1 handful of raisins
OPTIONAL:
1 tsp mustard
125ml brown beer
1 tbsp tomato puree
1 splash genever or cognac

—— Ask the butcher for 4 thin (5mm) slices of veal or beef fillet, about 12-15cm long and 8-10cm wide. If they are too thick, they can be thinned by wrapping them in cling film and pounding them with a meat cleaver or rolling pin.

—— Mix together 2 slices of bread soaked in 100ml of milk, the minced meat and a beaten egg, flavoured with a finely chopped shallot, a handful of the mushrooms thinly sliced and a level teaspoon of sage. You can also add a teaspoon of mustard and a splash of cognac or genever.

—— Roll a fistful of filling in each thin steak slice before folding over the edges to form little barrel-shaped parcels that need to be tied tightly with twine or kitchen string.

—— In a frying pan, brown the parcels on all sides in a mixture of butter and oil. When done, set them aside in a saucepan. Fry up the remaining sliced or quartered mushrooms, then add to the saucepan with the parcels. Fry 2 thinly sliced shallots and a crushed clove of garlic for 5 minutes, then add the diced carrots. Cook for a further 5 minutes on a high heat. Add the vegetables to the saucepan. Then deglaze the frying pan with the stock, and add it to the saucepan with the raisins, a bay leaf and a level teaspoon of thyme. For a richer sauce you can add half a bottle of brown beer. Bring the saucepan to the boil then simmer for 30 minutes on a medium-low heat.

—— Before serving, place the meat parcels in a warm dish and cover with tinfoil. Thicken the sauce with a tablespoon of flour mixed with water and stir it through well. If the sauce thickens too much it can be thinned out with beer, cream or milk. Flavour the sauce with the juice of a lemon, a tablespoon of tomato puree (optional) and a handful of chopped parsley.

ⓘ Serve with boiled potatoes or *stoemp* and Brussels sprouts or braised chicory.

Liège-style
MEATBALLS

4 servings

**1 frying pan
or deep-fat fryer**

1 large saucepan

1 mixing bowl

50 minutes

600g minced pork and beef

4 medium onions

100g breadcrumbs

150ml milk

2 eggs

2 glugs of vegetable oil

6 tbsp *sirop de Liège*

(or 4 tbsp redcurrant jelly

and 2 tbsp honey)

50g sugar

6 bay leaves

100ml white vinegar

2 tbsp butter

2 tbsp flour

OPTIONAL:

1 handful of currants

— In a large mixing bowl, beat the eggs into the milk, then add a finely chopped onion, the breadcrumbs and minced meat. Mix the ingredients by hand then divide it into 8 balls, or *boulets*, each about the size of a tennis ball.

— The *boulets* can be cooked in a deep-fat fryer or a frying pan. For the deep-fat fryer option, use beef fat and cook the round *boulets* for 10 minutes at 180°C. If pan-frying, flatten the *boulets* to a thickness of 4-5cm (like small, plump burgers) and cook them in oil for 10-15 minutes, turning regularly. Then add 150ml of water, cover and cook on a low heat for a further 10 minutes.

— Once cooked, set the *boulets* and their juices aside on a plate or in a bowl. Use the hot frying pan to cook 3 roughly chopped onions in oil for 10 minutes. When they start turning brown, add half a cup of vinegar to the onions and scrape up the burnt sugars from the bottom of the pan. Transfer the contents of the frying pan to a large saucepan and add 500ml of water, the sugar, *sirop de Liège* (or its replacement) and bay leaves. Bring to the boil before turning the heat down to a gentle simmer for 5-10 minutes.

— In the frying pan over a low heat, melt 2 tablespoons of butter mixed with 2 tablespoons of flour. Stir and remove from the heat half a minute after the butter melts so that none of the flour burns. Add a cup of the sauce to this roux and mix until smooth, then return to the saucepan and stir it in. When the sauce starts to thicken, add the *boulets* and cook for a further 10 minutes.

These meatballs are traditionally served with a blond beer, chips, mayonnaise and a simple lettuce salad.

A coarse or medium minced meat will make nicer *boulets* than finely minced meat.

People with a sweet tooth will appreciate the addition of a generous handful of currants, which can be added to the saucepan at the same time as the onions and water.

Hunting season

THE BELGIAN CULINARY DIARY CHANGES WITH THE SEASONS AND THE arrival of autumn means just one thing in Belgian kitchens: it's time to start enjoying venison, wild boar and pheasant. Hunting is strictly regulated in Belgium, both with regards to what can be hunted and when. While the exact dates of the hunting season vary from one game species to another and from one region to another, the season generally begins in September or October and it is a time of year eagerly awaited by most Belgians.

A couple of weeks before the season opens, the meat counters at supermarkets start to fill up with leaflets full of ideas for cooking game and shelves are cleared to make way for the wild mushrooms, chestnut puree and cranberries that are typically served with these dishes. Restaurants change their menus to reflect the season's cuisine and hotels in the Ardennes region offer autumn breaks promoting local food and walks in the forests.

SAINT HUBERT

To really sense the excitement and buzz about the hunting season, the place to go is Saint-Hubert, a village in the Ardennes named after the patron saint of hunting. Every year on Saint Hubert's day, November 3, the village celebrates the feast day with mass at the Basilica, followed by the blessing of the animals on the square in front of the building. The Royal-Forêt Saint-Hubert musicians play a fanfare, the horn players blow the hunting

horn and then the hunt is off. Celebrations continue in the village with a procession of floats and people dressed up in historical costumes, a local market and food and drink tastings.

Wild game and, increasingly, animals bred on game farms are found throughout the Ardennes, not just around Saint-Hubert but also places such as La Roche, Orval and Durbuy. Heading further east is the Eifel low mountain range in the German-speaking part of Belgium where game is an important part of the culinary tradition. Eastern Belgium is also home to the *Hertogenwald*, literally the Duke's forest, and appropriately enough home to one of the Crown Hunting Grounds. As to the Belgian monarchy's private Royal Hunting Ground, this is in the grounds of Ciergnon Castle, also in the Ardennes, not far from Rochefort.

While the most popular types of game found at the butchers and on restaurant menus in Belgium are venison, wild boar and pheasant, the range also includes partridge, hare and wild rabbit. These animals, famously depicted in still lifes by 16th and 17th century Flemish painters such as Frans Snyders, have been hunted and eaten for centuries. Whereas in the past, game was predominantly for rich landowners who would go hunting on their land, today it is much more widely available. The meat can be prepared in numerous ways, including roasted, as fillets or in stews. Smoked meats, pâtés and terrines are also common ways of preparing game.

Pheasant *à la Brabançonne* is about as Belgian a game dish as it's possible to get, with the pheasant accompanied by the most classic of local vegetables, chicory. It is also the perfect example of how side dishes are an integral part of the overall dish. [→ see recipe p.128]

As for sauces, a popular one is the mushroom-based hunters' sauce (*sauce chasseur* in French and *jagerssaus* in Dutch), which is nowadays not only served with game but also meatballs and other dishes. Particularly Belgian preparations to accompany game are sauces made from Gueuze beer or genever spirit or other favourites such as juniper berries, sweet chestnuts or wild mushrooms.

WILD BOAR
with chestnut sauce

🍴 4 servings

🍴 1 roasting tin
1 frying pan
1 small saucepan

🕐 Preparation: 35 minutes
Cooking: 18-25 minutes

600g thick wild boar fillet
2 knobs of butter
12 shallots
200ml game stock
100ml milk
200g chestnut purée
1 splash of cognac
1 tsp or 1 sprig of thyme
1 bay leaf
Salt & pepper

— Fry the whole peeled shallots for 5 minutes in butter, then set aside in a roasting tin and brown the whole fillet of wild boar on all sides in a generous knob of butter. Put the meat in the roasting tin, then deglaze the frying pan with ¾ of the stock, making sure to scrape up the sweet flavoursome sugars that are attached to the bottom of the pan. Add a pinch of salt, a turn of pepper, thyme and a bay leaf, then pour over the meat.

— Place the roasting tin in a pre-heated oven at 200°C for 18-25 minutes. The meat should still be pink, tender and a touch undercooked when you remove it from the oven. Transfer the meat and the shallots to a plate and cover with aluminium foil while you prepare the sauce. Be aware that the meat will continue to cook under its aluminium tent.

THE SAUCE:

— Pour the remaining 50ml of stock into the roasting tin, mix well with the cooking juices and then pour through a sieve into a small saucepan. Add the chestnut purée, milk and a splash of cognac, and bring to the boil. Leave it to simmer gently for 5 minutes, stirring regularly so that it creates a smooth sauce.

— Serve the wild boar in slices, covered in sauce and accompanied by the shallots.

ⓘ Boar pairs well with a combination of of the following: celeriac or parsnip *stoemp*, roast salsify or pumpkin, whole roast sweet chestnuts or hazelnuts, Jerusalem artichokes or turnips, onion marmalade or cranberry jelly, pears cooked in red wine or grilled figs with honey, pan-fried wild mushrooms and stewed redcurrants.

ⓘ The best cuts of boar for this recipe are boneless shoulder, hindshanks and tenderloin. In Belgium, fresh young wild boar called *mannetjesvarken/marcassin* are easy to find during the autumn and winter hunting season, and are available frozen in most large supermarkets throughout the year. Elsewhere, wild boar is often available on request from local butchers.

ⓘ In Belgium a deep, rich game stock is sold in jars in most supermarkets, labelled as *'wildfond/fond de gibier'*. If this is unavailable, use a strong pork, chicken or mushroom stock.

Brabant-style PHEASANT

4 servings

1 large frying pan
1 earthenware pot
or baking tray
with a tinfoil lid
1 saucepan

Preparation: 1 hour
Cooking: 45 minutes

2 whole pheasants
8-12 chicory
6 slices bacon
2 tsp sugar
250ml chicken stock
200ml beer
200ml fresh cream
1 large knob of butter
1 splash of oil
1 tbsp cornflour
1 tsp nutmeg
15 crushed coriander seeds
Pepper
300g stuffing

— Remove any damaged chicory leaves and scoop out the core from the base of each head. Cook in 2 batches in a pan with a large knob of butter for about 10 minutes per batch. Halfway through the cooking of each batch, add half a teaspoon of ground nutmeg and a teaspoon of sugar. Don't overcook.

— Place the chicory around the inside of an earthenware pot with a lid or a deep baking tray that can be covered with tinfoil.

— Wash and dry the pheasants, then trim off the butter-coloured fat. Fry the birds on all sides in a splash of oil to seal the skin before setting aside to cool. To keep the white meat moist, stuff the cavities with a mix of flavoursome ingredients as detailed below, then cover the breasts with the the slices of bacon and a piece of tinfoil.

— Place the dressed birds in the centre of the cooking pot surrounded by the chicory and add the crushed coriander seeds, a generous turn of the pepper grinder and ⅔ of the flavoured chicken stock, which should come about a centimetre or two up the birds. Cover the pot or baking tray with a lid or tinfoil and place in a pre-heated oven at 200°C for 45 minutes.

— About 15 minutes before serving, heat the remaining third of chicken stock in a saucepan with 200ml of beer. Allow it to reduce over a high heat for 5 minutes before adding a heaped teaspoon of cornflour mixed into half a glass of water. Turn the heat down to medium and stir regularly as the sauce thickens. 5 minutes before serving, add 200ml of cream and turn the heat down to low. Just before serving, stir the cooking juices from the pheasants and chicory into the sauce and pour this directly onto the plates or serve separately in a sauce jug.

It is traditional to serve the pheasant breast as a first serving and the tougher legs as a second serving. This dish can be accompanied with croquettes or sprout *stoemp*, celeriac puree, roast parsnips, steamed carrots or salsify, roast chestnuts and a lamb's lettuce salad.

The stuffing is a mix which can include walnuts, breadcrumbs soaked in milk, butter beans, sultanas, a finely chopped apple, leek, thyme, Ardennes ham, chopped blood sausage and a spoonful of honey.

For the love of chicken

ONE OF THE NICKNAMES FOR THE PEOPLE OF BRUSSELS IS *Kiekenfretters*, a word in local dialect that literally means 'chicken gobblers'. The name may derive quite simply from the fact that citizens of Brussels and the surrounding areas eat a lot of chicken. There are also more interesting versions of its origins.

One account is that the Flemish, after defeating Brussels in the battle of Scheut five centuries ago, entered the Brussels army barracks and discovered large quantities of chicken. Another refers to how in the 14th century the people of Brussels attacked Gaasbeek castle to avenge the death of Everard t'Serclaes, a hero whose statue can today be found on the Grand' Place in Brussels. Upon entering the castle, the people of Brussels are said to have plundered and eaten all the chickens. Whatever the truth, the nickname *Kiekenfretters* has stuck.

While the people of Brussels may be known for their love of eating chicken, Londerzeel, some 20 kilometres north of the capital, has other connections with the bird. Every September, the Flemish town organises an event known as the 'Golden Throwing of Chicken Leg' (*Gouden Kiekenpootworp*) where some 2,500 chicken legs are thrown from the windows of the town hall into the crowd gathered below. The person to catch the first chicken leg wins a piece of gold jewellery,

while another 250 get a roast chicken. The town hall also boasts a bronze statue of a chicken leg, which each year is dressed up in a different costume. These unique festivities aim to highlight the area's long and proud history of chicken farming.

MECHELEN CUCKOO

The Flemish town of Mechelen is also proud of its avian past, having been one of the world's most important chicken suppliers in the mid-19th century. This success began to wane at the start of the 20th century and it wasn't until the early 1990s that Mechelen was back on the chicken map. Its reversal of fortune came about when small poultry farmers realised that there was renewed demand for quality chicken.

Today in Belgium the Mechelen chicken is considered one of the highest quality birds and is famed for its firm, tender meat. Somewhat confusingly for foreigners the chicken is called *Mechelse Koekoek*, literally Mechelen Cuckoo. The only link with cuckoos, however, is that the breed has cuckoo-coloured feathers. This Mechelen specialty can be prepared in many ways and is a staple on restaurant menus throughout the region.

Chicken dishes that appear regularly on Belgian brasserie menus are *vol-au-vents*, chicken *waterzooi*, chicken croquettes and roast chicken and chips served with apple sauce.

Vol-au-vents, individual puff pastry cases with a savoury filling, have found their way into Belgian cooking from France, where they are known as *bouchée à la reine* ('the Queen's mouthful'). This name is a nod to Louis xv's wife Maria Leszcynska, the Queen of France, who is said to have come up with the idea of the individual portions in the 18th century. The chef Marie-Antoine Carême later adapted the recipe, using a lighter pastry. The name *vol-au-vent* is attributed to him; meaning 'windblown', it refers to the lightness of the pastry.

    Waterzooi on the other hand is 100% Belgian. Part stew, part hearty soup, it can be made with either fish or chicken. The dish is thought to have originated in the river-port town of Ghent and to have first been made with fish but as the waterways became polluted the fish was replaced with chicken. Today the dish is more commonly made with chicken and is often referred to as Ghent *waterzooi*.

It may well be the people of Brussels who are called 'chicken gobblers' but in the last few decades chicken has become common fare for the whole nation.

Homemade
VOL-AU-VENT

Y⫩ 6 servings

/ 1 large saucepan

1 frying pan

1 medium saucepan

🕐 1½ -2 hours

1 chicken or partridge

500g puff pastry

200ml white wine

1 large carrot

1 medium onion

1 leek green

1 handful of celery leaves

1 lemon

250g white button mushrooms

300ml milk

50g flour

70g butter

2-3 garlic cloves

1 bay leaf

1 sprig or 1 tsp thyme

2 large handfuls of parsley

3 whole cloves

3 juniper berries

OPTIONAL:

150g minced meat

30g breadcrumbs

1 egg

200g veal escalope

1 sweetbread

COOKING THE BIRD:

— The dish requires a whole bird that is boiled on a bed of vegetables. Cut up a carrot, an onion, some leek and celery greens and place in a large saucepan. Prepare the bird by removing its skin, stuffing it with a whole peeled lemon studded with 3 cloves, then place on top of the vegetables. Cover with cold water and add a clove of garlic, juniper berries (or a teaspoon of gin or genever if these are unavailable), white wine, a bay leaf, thyme and a couple of sprigs of parsley. Bring to a gentle boil and simmer for 50 minutes.

THE PASTRY CASES:

— Store-bought vol-au-vent cases are often very good. However, if you choose to make your own, roll out 500g of puff pastry [→ store-bought or homemade following the recipe on p.210] on a lightly floured surface and fold it over until it is 1cm deep. Using a pastry cutter or a sharp knife dipped in flour, cut the pastry into circles or squares about the diameter of your palm. Score each case with the blunt edge of a knife about 1cm from the edge to form a lid. Be careful not to cut all the way through as this will damage the base of the cases. Brush with milk to glaze and place in a pre-heated oven at 230°C for 10-15 minutes. The cases will rise and take on a beautiful golden brown colour. Cool on a wire rack before removing the lid with a sharp knife and scooping out any excess uncooked pastry from the centre with a spoon.

THE FILLING:

— Remove the chicken and set aside to cool. Keep the cooking stock to make the sauce.

— A second meat is often added to vol-au-vents and is cooked in this stock. This meat can be diced veal escalopes, sweetbreads or little balls (1cm in diameter) made of minced veal, pork or beef mixed with breadcrumbs and an egg.

— The veal escalopes will need to be simmered in the stock at a moderate heat for 15 minutes, while the meatballs and sweetbreads will only require 3-4 minutes. The meatballs are ready when they float up to the surface. The sweetbreads will benefit from being soaked in several changes of cold water

· · · →

for a few hours before being simmered gently in the stock. When you take them out, allow them to cool then trim off any sinew or gristle and slice. When you are plating the dish they can be reheated in the béchamel sauce or lightly dusted in flour or breadcrumbs and pan-fried.

—— Fry 250g of cleaned and quartered white button mushrooms in a knob of butter with a clove or two of garlic until brown. Set aside while you debone and shred the chicken into pieces.

—— To make the béchamel sauce, gently heat 50g of flour in a saucepan for half a minute, then add 50g of butter and mix into a fine paste. Add 300ml of the warm cooking stock and 300ml of milk. Whisk vigorously so that there are no lumps and then again regularly as the sauce thickens. About 5 minutes before serving, add the chicken, partner meat, mushrooms and a large handful of finely chopped parsley.

—— Spoon the filling into the pastry cases and place the cases' lids on top of the filling. Garnish with any remaining filling and a few chervil or parsley leaves.

○
Accompany with steamed spinach leaves flavoured with fried shallots, lightly steamed cauliflower and couscous made with the remaining cooking stock, rice or fries.

○
Vol-au-vents can be prepared up to 24 hours in advance, refrigerated and heated through in an oven at 200°C for 8-10 minutes.

○
Smaller quantities of vol-au-vents can be made from the leftovers of a roast chicken. When doing this, squeeze the juice of half a lemon over the meat to give it a less greasy and fresher taste.

○
A delicious vegetarian version of this dish can be prepared with tofu fried with onion and mushrooms and a béchamel sauce flavoured with tarragon and nutmeg. Accompany with a celery and rocket salad, chopped walnuts, cubes of pear fried in sunflower oil, blue cheese, and olive or mushroom tapenade.

Ghent
WATERZOOI

🍴 4-6 servings

🍳 1 frying pan

1 large Dutch oven

1 small saucepan

1 large bowl

1 small bowl

🕐 1½ -2 hours

1 chicken

1½ litres stock

2 egg yolks

200ml cream

1 lemon

4 large or 6 medium
or 12 new potatoes

2 medium onions

2 garlic cloves

3 large carrots

¼ celeriac

1 large leek

3 sticks celery

2 large sprigs of parsley

1 bay leaf

½ tsp thyme

2 cloves

10 peppercorns

4 juniper berries

1 small pinch of cayenne pepper

1 tsp nutmeg

1 splash of vegetable oil

—— Fry 2 thinly sliced onions and 2 sliced cloves of garlic in a splash of oil for 5 minutes, then transfer them to a heavy-bottomed saucepan and add the bay leaf, thyme, half the parsley, the cloves, peppercorns, juniper berries and cayenne pepper.

—— Wash and trim the fat off your chicken and put the bird in the pot with the onions, herbs and spices. A whole chicken is best, but you can use smaller pieces. If you prepare the dish with smaller pieces, cook the brown meat for 15 minutes longer than the white meat.

—— Pour 1-1½ litres of stock into the pot [→ see 🗒 on the next page]. The stock should cover about ⅔ of the chicken. This will enable the drumsticks and thighs to cook in the stock and the breast to cook in the steam. Cover and simmer on a low heat for about an hour, until the meat starts to fall off the bone.

—— Peel the potatoes and celeriac and then cut the potatoes into bite-size chunks (unless you're using small, new potatoes in which case you can leave them as they are). Dice the celeriac and squeeze over the juice of half a lemon to help keep the white colour. Set aside.

—— Chop the white of the leek, the carrots and celery into small pieces. Put them in a saucepan of salted boiling water for 3 minutes and then remove with a slotted spoon and drop in a large bowl of cold water. Set aside until 5-10 minutes before serving.

—— Once the chicken is cooked, remove it from the pot and place on a chopping board. At the same time, put the potatoes and celeriac into the pot and adjust the heat so that the stock is gently boiling. As soon as the chicken is cool enough to touch, remove the bones and skin and either discard them or keep them to make a stock later. Shred the meat into bite-size pieces.

—— When the potatoes and celeriac are cooked, return the meat to the pot along with the colourful vegetables and a teaspoon of nutmeg. Turn the heat down to a gentle simmer. Lightly beat 2 egg yolks with 200ml of cream. Pour this into the stock and mix well. Don't let the liquid boil as it will curdle.

· · · →

—— A couple of minutes after having added the cream and egg yolks, serve the waterzooi in heated bowls and accompany with crusty brown bread. A couple of drops of lemon juice and a sprinkle of finely chopped parsley will complete this dish perfectly.

⸮ An old hen that is unsuitable for roasting makes a better waterzooi than a young roasting bird: the tough meat is much more flavoursome, although it will take about 10-15 minutes longer to cook.

⸮ A key ingredient in this dish is the stock. A good vegetable stock can be made by chopping and frying an onion, along with a carrot, the green tops of a leek and a stick of celery. Crushed garlic, peppercorns, bay leaves and the stems and damaged leaves of a bunch of parsley all add further flavour. Pour in 1.5 litres of water, bring to the boil and leave to simmer for 30 minutes. For a chicken stock, boil the bones of a chicken and add vegetables, herbs and spices as above; freeze and defrost when needed.

The cheese-board

B ELGIUM IS RARELY THOUGHT OF AS A MAJOR CHEESE-PRODUCING country and yet it has more than 300 varieties, a figure that rivals that of France. The reason Belgian cheeses are not as well-known as their French counterparts is quite simply because many are only produced in small quantities and much of Belgium's cheese stays in the country rather than being exported.

So what would you find on a good Belgian cheeseboard? At least one hard or semi-hard cheese, a soft cheese, a blue cheese and a goat's cheese are all essentials in order to reflect the main cheese groups found nationwide.

Many of Belgium's hard and semi-hard cheeses have links with an abbey, for example Maredsous, Chimay or Grimbergen, and are often enjoyed with a beer from the same abbey. In some cases, beer is actually used in the production of the cheese. Take for example Chimay *à la bière*, a cheese whose natural rind is washed in Chimay Trappist beer, adding an aroma of hops to its apricot-peach taste.

The prize for the smelliest cheese has to go to Herve, a soft cheese with washed rind from the Belgian region of the same name. This region is exceptionally proud of its cheese, which can only be made in these climatic and agricultural conditions. In fact the cheese's specificity has earned it the Protected Designation of Origin label. The locals' pride also stems from the cheese's history. Herve cheese, which dates back to the Middle Ages, really started to flourish in the 16th century when the Holy Roman Emperor Charles v banned the export of wheat grains, a move that resulted in local farmers switching from growing grains to breeding dairy cows and producing cheese. Hundreds of years later and the tradition is still going strong.

Another interesting cheese from this region is the Remoudou, a soft cheese made from raw cow milk. The rind is washed in salty water before the final washing in a strong beer. This cheese also dates back to the Middle Ages, when farmers used it as a means of paying the landowner. Its name comes from the Walloon word *rimoude*, which literally means 're-milk', i.e. using the milk from a second milking.

There are also cream cheeses such as *maquée* in Wallonia and *plattekaas* in Flanders. *Maquée* (which derives from the Walloon word for curd or cream cheese) and *plattekaas* (which literally means 'flat cheese') have a mild taste and are often mixed with horseradish, chopped onions, radishes and/or herbs such as fresh chives or parsley. Brussels Cheese, which is sometimes mistakenly confused with these cream cheeses, is in fact a fermented cheese with a sharp and citrus taste. Finding the genuine article, however, can be a tall order these days.

For blue cheeses, you could try the prize-winning Achel Blue from Limburg, the Bleu des Moines from Herve, or the Pas de Bleu from Flemish organic cheese cooperative Het Hinkelspel.

COOKING WITH CHEESE

As well as eating cheeses cold with a chunk of bread or as an accompaniment to beer, Belgians also enjoy cooking with cheese, for example in a sauce, as a gratin such as *chicons au gratin* [→ see the section on vegetables, p.94], between two layers of toast as a *croque monsieur* or between two pancakes in what is known as a *double*, in salads, quiches, cheese croquettes or even in desserts such as *mattentaart/tarte au maton* [→ see the section on desserts, p.172].

Many towns have their specialty, such as Nivelles and its *tarte al djote*, a quiche-like dish whose two ingredients are *djote* (chard), which gives it its deep green colour, and a local cheese called Boulette de Nivelles or Bètchéye. It is not known exactly when the *tarte al djote* recipe was first used, but some believe it was served to Emperor Henry III at the consecration of Nivelles Abbey in 1046. The Flemish town of Aalst is known for its onion tart, which as well as lots of onions is also made with smoked bacon and grated cheese, and Dinant prides itself on its *flamiche* made with Boulette de Romedenne cheese, eggs and butter.

The Boulette cheeses deserve a special mention as at the time of writing they were being considered for the Protected Geographical Indication (PGI) designation. The PGI application included seven varieties: Boulette de Nivelles or Bètchéye; Boulette or Cassette de Beaumont; Boulette de Surice; Boulette de Romedenne; Boulette de Falaën; Boulette de Namur or Crau Stofé; and Boulette de Huy. All of these are traditional Walloon soft cheeses made from skimmed raw cow milk from farms in their region. The classic shape of a boulette cheese is, as the name suggests, a little ball, though it is also found in a flattened or conical shape.

Ardennes goats' cheese QUICHE

4 servings

1 baking tin (25-30cm)

1 mixing bowl

1 frying pan

1 saucepan

1 small bowl

Preparation: 30 minutes

Refrigeration: 30 minutes

Cooking: 40 minutes

FOR THE BASE:

200g plain white flour

75g soft butter

100ml single or double cream

1 tsp sugar

1 egg

1 large pinch of salt

FOR THE FILLING:

180g firm goats' cheese

200g fromage frais

1 large handful of celery leaves

300g frozen or 1kg fresh

spinach (without cream)

1 large (± 200g) leek white

200g wild (or button)

mushrooms

4 large eggs

1 sprig or 1tsp thyme

1 tsp chopped fresh

or dried chives

1 tsp celery salt

1 pinch of pepper

THE BASE:

— Mix the soft butter, cream, egg, sugar and salt in a bowl and sieve in the flour a quarter at a time. Stir the mixture well so that it is smooth before putting in the fridge for 30 minutes. When it has hardened, roll it out on a lightly floured surface to a thickness of half a centimetre and the diameter of your pie tin, plus 2cm of crust on each side. Transfer the base to a greased baking tin and blind bake (cover the base of the dough with a piece of greaseproof paper and put a handful of baking beans on top) in a pre-heated oven at 180°C for 15 minutes.

THE FILLING :

— Chop and fry the mushrooms, the thinly sliced leek white and the roughly chopped light green celery leaves in a pan with a little oil for 10 minutes. If using fresh spinach leaves, steam them in a saucepan with a little water for 10 minutes. If using frozen spinach, let them defrost over a low heat.

— Beat the eggs with the pepper, thyme, chives, celery salt and then stir in the fromage frais. Drain the spinach, then squeeze it to push out any excess liquid, and scatter it evenly over the base of the quiche. Cover this with the mushrooms, leeks and celery leaves, then the egg mixture and top with diced pieces of goats' cheese. Return to the oven at 200°C for 30 minutes, then turn the heat down to 160°C and cook for a further 10 minutes.

Ardennes goats' cheese quiche is best accompanied by a rocket and lamb's lettuce salad mixed with sliced radishes and spring onions.

Spinach leaves can be replaced or complemented by sorrel leaves, which will bring a sour lemony tang to the quiche, or by the torn leaves and roughly chopped stems of vibrantly coloured, bitter-tasting chard.

CROQUE
Monsieur

1 serving

1 frying pan
or sandwich toaster

10 minutes

2 slices of sweet sandwich
bread
1 slice of semi-hard cheese
1 slice of ham
Butter
OPTIONAL:
1 egg

— A traditional Belgian croque is made with fresh sweet sandwich bread (sold as *pain de mie/toastbrood* in Belgium). Flavoursome semi-hard cheese such as Herve, Maredsous or Chimay forms the first layer of the filling and wet-cured pink ham or air-dried *jambon d'Ardenne* makes the second.

— Unlike a traditional sandwich, a croque is buttered on the outside of both slices of bread. It is put in a hot frying pan or a sandwich toaster until the bread is golden brown and crunchy. If fried in a pan, press down on the croque with a spatula from time to time.

— A croque can be served with a fried egg and changes name to Croque Madame. This is one of many inventive variations on this dish which include:

- Yucatan: guacamole + sweetcorn + chorizo
- Rajasthan: grilled chicken + curry sauce + fresh mango + fresh coriander
- Svenska: smoked salmon + salmon tartare + fresh dill + lemon zest + pepper
- Adriatico: gorgonzola + parma ham + marinated sun-dried tomatoes + parmesan
- Italiano: mozzarella + parmesan + grilled courgettes + grilled peppers
- Français: grilled chicken + fried leek + rosemary + gruyère
- British: cheddar + bacon + mushrooms + fried onions
- Marrakech: minced lamb + ras el hanout + aubergine + goats' cheese
- Popeye: spinach + goats' cheese + oregano

— Croques can be prepared in advance and reheated in a hot oven for 5 minutes. Serve cut into halves or quarters, from corner to corner.

ⓘ A deluxe version of a croque is to fry it in the pan, then put it on a piece of tinfoil, cover it in béchamel sauce [→ see the recipe for braised chicory on p.94] and grated parmesan cheese, and put it under the grill for 5 minutes.

Heavenly bread

B ELGIANS LOVE THEIR BAKERIES. EVEN TODAY WHEN BREAD IS WIDELY available in supermarkets, Belgians prefer to go to their local bakery. And it's easy to understand why: as soon as you walk in, the aroma of freshly baked bread wafts over you while your eyes simply feast on the wide choice before you.

The bakery is the place to buy croissants and *pains au chocolat*, bread rolls and baguettes, brioche breads such as *cramique* or *craquelin* and often cakes too. It is also of course the place to buy loaves of bread, which range from pure white to dark brown, come in a range of shapes from square and rectangular to round and oval, and are made from a variety of grains including wheat, rye and spelt. The broad range reflects Belgium's own baking traditions as well as influences from neighbouring France and Germany.

The bakery is also a part of the local community in Belgium, no matter whether you live in a village or a city. And if there's one day when the visit to the bakers is sacred, it's Sunday, when Belgians like to buy a selection of breads and pastries for breakfast or brunch. Breakfast may be a rushed affair during the week, but on Sunday everything happens at a slower pace, starting with a lingering breakfast of breads served with butter and jam, chocolate spread or cheese. A basket of croissants, *pains au chocolat* and *couques aux raisins* (raisin buns) almost always finds its way onto the breakfast table too.

This experience is replicated at one of Belgium's best-known chains of bakery-cum-café, Le Pain Quotidien, which means Daily Bread. Founded by the Belgian chef Alain Coumont in 1990, Le Pain Quotidien has expanded

from its first shop in Rue Antoine Dansaert in Brussels to more than 100 outlets worldwide today. Of course Le Pain Quotidien doesn't just open its doors on Sunday mornings but is open throughout the week.

As far as a quick lunch is concerned, a white or brown baguette filled with cheese, meat or fish and salad is a popular choice. Other breads frequently used for making sandwiches are the *pistolet*, a white bread roll that has a crunchy crust on the outside and is soft on the inside, and small milk rolls that are aptly called *pain sandwich*.

For breads to accompany a meal, there are no hard and fast rules although the Walloon Agency for the Promotion of Quality Agriculture makes the following suggestions: white bread goes well with simple dishes; wholemeal bread works well with cold meats; for a cheeseboard nut bread is a good choice; rye bread complements seafood well; and brioche goes well with foie gras.

As well as savoury breads, Belgium is also proud of its sweeter breads such as gingerbread (known as *pain d'épices* by the Francophones and *peperkoek* by the Flemish speakers), *cougnou*, *cramique* (*kramiek* or *rozijnenbrood* for the Flemish) and *craquelin* (or *suikerbrood*).

Gingerbread is made with flour and honey, is halfway between cake and bread, and is eaten as a snack in slices either on its own or spread with butter. *Cougnou* is a small sweet raisin bread in the shape of a swaddled baby Jesus that is traditionally baked at Christmas time. As for *cramique* and *craquelin*, these are both varieties of brioche breads and go particularly well with a mug of hot chocolate on a rainy day. Cramique is a rectangular loaf of raisin bread while craquelin has small pearls of sugar rather than raisins.

TRADITIONS WITH BREAD

Bread is also a central feature of many celebrations. To mark the feast day of Saint Hubert, the patron saint of hunting and also the saint invoked for protection against rabies, on November 3 many bakeries sell round bread buns some of which have raisins in, others aniseed or cinnamon. In the town of Ghent they are known as *mastellen*. Whatever their name, the Christian tradition is to have the bread rolls blessed to help prevent rabies.

In the Flemish village of Elst, it is traditional to bake flatbread in communal ovens for the feast of Saint Apollonia in early February. During the celebration, known as the *Geutelingen* festival after the name of the flatbread, visitors to Elst can buy this traditional bread fresh from the oven.

Perhaps the best known bread-related celebration is one recognised by UNESCO: *Krakelingenfeest* in the Flemish town of Geraardsbergen. The festival includes a parade through the town at the end of which thousands of special ring-shaped breads called *krakelingen* are thrown into the crowd. The festive ritual celebrates the end of winter.

CRAMIQUE

2 loaves

1 large bowl

2 small bowls

2 bread tins or baking tins

Preparation: 40 minutes

Standing: 2 hours

Cooking: 40-45 minutes

550g plain flour

3 eggs

20g fresh yeast

250g raisins

100g brown sugar

100g soft butter

150ml milk

150ml warm water

1 large pinch of cinnamon

— In a small bowl, stir the fresh yeast and sugar into the milk and warm water until the yeast has dissolved. Add a couple of tablespoons of flour and stir until smooth, then set aside for 15 minutes.

— Sieve the remaining flour into a large bowl and mix in a generous pinch of cinnamon and the raisins. Lightly beat 2 of the 3 eggs and add to the small bowl containing the yeast.

— Stir the liquid and dry ingredients together using either the paddle attachment of an electronic mixer on a slow setting, or gently and gradually by hand. If you are mixing manually, this is best achieved by digging a well in the middle of the flour and filling it with a third of the liquid at a time, drawing the dry mixture in from the edges to the middle until smooth.

— The dough must now be allowed to double in size. Leave it in a warm place covered with cling film or a tea towel for about an hour.

— Once doubled in size, dice the 100g of soft butter and knead it into the dough. As you do this the dough will reduce in size and make a popping sound as the gases are forced out.

— Transfer the dough to greased bread tins or baking tins, filling them no more than halfway, then cover with cling film or a tea towel, and leave in a warm place for about an hour in order to rise again.

— Once risen, gently push the dough back into the tins to force out any large air pockets and then lightly brush with some beaten egg.

— Place in the middle of a pre-heated oven at 180°C for 40-45 minutes.

— There are 2 ways to check if a cramique is cooked: tap the top with a knife handle and if the loaf sounds hollow then it is ready, or insert a skewer into the centre of the cramique and if it comes out clean then it's ready. Once cooked, remove the cramique from the tin and leave to cool on a wire rack.

ⓘ Cramique is best eaten a few hours after it has come out of the oven. It can be kept for several days in a paper bag in the fridge, and if it becomes dry then it is delicious toasted.

ⓘ Make your raisins and sultanas moist and plump by soaking them in water or tea for a few hours or boiling them for 15 minutes. This will make the cramique tastier and help it stay fresh for longer.

Fresh GINGERBREAD

1 loaf

1 mixing bowl

1 saucepan

1 bread tin

Preparation: 15 minutes

Cooking: 40-45 minutes

250ml milk

250g plain flour

125g caster sugar

8 tbsp honey

1 tsp cinnamon

4 tsp ground ginger

1 tsp ground star anise

2 tsp bicarbonate of soda

OPTIONAL:

1 tsp fresh ginger

1 handful of pearl sugar
and/or candied ginger

— In a saucepan or microwave, warm the milk for a few minutes, to body temperature, and then add the honey and ground ginger. Warming the milk helps the honey and ginger to diffuse evenly.

— Mix the flour, sugar, cinnamon, star anise and bicarbonate of soda in a bowl and stir in the sweetened milk a quarter at a time. The mixture will take on the consistency of a thick batter.

— Pour the mixture into a greased or lined bread tin and place in a pre-heated oven at 180°C for 40-45 minutes. The best test to see if it is cooked is to insert a skewer into the gingerbread; if it comes out clean then it's ready.

— Once cooked, remove from the tin and leave to cool on a wire rack. Serve in slices as afternoon tea or in lunchboxes.

A teaspoon of freshly chopped or grated ginger can be added to the recipe to make the ginger bread spicier. Peeling ginger is easiest using a spoon instead of a knife or peeler.

A handful of pearl sugar and/or candied ginger can be sprinkled over the gingerbread after it has been in the oven for 30 minutes.

Waffles and pancakes

BELGIANS ARE PASSIONATE ABOUT THEIR WAFFLES, WHICH THE Francophones call *gaufres* and the Flemish *wafels*. Walk down a cobbled street, across a park or through a fair almost anywhere in the country and you'll be sure to smell the distinctive aroma of sugary waffles wafting your way from a nearby stand. It's one of those smells that means 'home' to a Belgian.

There are two main types, the Brussels waffle and the Liège waffle. It is the latter that is most commonly sold at stands and eaten on the go, whereas the former is more likely to be found in a café or restaurant and enjoyed sitting on a terrace. The most immediate distinction between the two is their shape: the Brussels waffle is perfectly rectangular, while its Liège counterpart has uneven edges. The more important distinction, however, is the taste and texture.

The Liège waffle is chunkier and more filling, with its chief characteristic pearl sugar, a pure white sugar that doesn't immediately melt at high temperatures and so spreads through to the surface of the waffle where it crystallizes. These waffles are usually eaten plain, but if you're feeling indulgent you can always ask for a bit of chocolate to be slipped in the middle. Brussels waffles, in contrast, are of a lighter consistency, fluffier and almost transparent in colour. Offsetting their lightness are the many possible toppings with which they can be served, from a dusting of icing sugar to whipped cream and strawberries.

In fact it was a Brussels waffle served with strawberries and whipped cream that was the first to travel to the other side of the Atlantic. The introduction of the Belgian waffle in the United States took place at New York's World Fair in 1964 when Maurice Vermersch, a businessman and waffle-maker from Brussels, took his wares to the global fair and sold them under the name of 'Bel-Gem Waffles'.

No matter which type of waffle we're talking about, they all have a distinctive honeycomb structure, which comes from the iron in which the batter is cooked. The importance of the waffle iron is underlined by Charles-Xavier Ménage, the curator of the small yet delightful Museum of Gastronomy in the Walloon village of Hermalle-sous-Huy. The iron is to the waffle-maker what the hammer is to the carpenter: the indispensable tool of the craft, says Ménage, proudly showing the centuries-old waffle irons on display in his museum.

Closely related to the waffle are the so-called *lacquemants* in the south of the country and *lukken* in the north. *Lacquemants* are traditionally sold as sweet snacks at fairs, in particular at Liège's big fair in October and end-of-year fairs. Thinner than a waffle, they have a criss-cross effect rather than honeycomb structure on their surface and are filled with a sugary syrup flavoured with orange blossom. As for *lukken*, they are a typical West Flemish snack often served at New Year (*lukken* means to wish someone good luck). A good description is found in a West Flemish dictionary dating from 1873, which describes the treat as a 'thin, solid little wafer, usually oval-shaped, and baked with flour, butter, and sugar'. The result is a delicious, buttery wafer that is crispy to the bite and then melts in your mouth.

PANCAKE TRADITIONS

The combination of flour and butter with various other ingredients is also commonly found in Belgium in the form of pancakes, which are as often savoury as sweet. One special occasion when pancakes are the order of the day is February 2, Candlemas in the Christian calendar, a celebration 40 days after the birth of Christ. While the candle-lit procession to church may not be so common today, the tradition of eating pancakes (known as *crêpes* in French and *pannenkoeken* in Flemish) has stuck.

There are many other dates throughout the year, often depending on the region, when pancakes are the traditional food. In Liège a pancake known as *bouquette Liègoise* is eaten at Christmas. It derives its name of *bouquette* from the buckwheat flour used to make it.

It is not just the flour that determines the pancake of course. There are also the flavourings and fillings. Several Belgian towns, such as Binche and Nivelles, make what they call *doubles*, two thin pancakes with a layer of cheese in between.

In Diest, what makes the pancakes special is tansy, a herb found in the area during spring. To celebrate the so-called *Diestse cruydtcoeck*, there is even a local group dedicated to the pancake, De Confrerie van den Cruydtcoeck, which aims to keep the centuries-old tradition alive.

Buckwheat
PANCAKES

10 pancakes

1 large mixing bowl

2 small bowls

1 small frying pan
(15-23cm diameter)

1 plate covered in tinfoil

Preparation: 20 minutes

Resting: 1 hour

Cooking: 30 minutes

FOR THE PANCAKES:

200g plain flour

100g buckwheat flour

25g fresh yeast

3 eggs

1 pinch of salt

1 heaped tbsp sugar

250ml warm milk

250ml water, beer or root beer

1 generous pinch of nutmeg

1 generous glug of sunflower oil

1 large knob of butter

FOR THE FILLING:

100g brown sugar

2 lemons

OPTIONAL:

1 small glass cognac (or rum)

3 large stewed apples

120g sultanas or raisins

— Crumble the yeast into a small bowl or pan containing the warm milk and add a heaped tablespoon of sugar and a pinch of salt. Give it a stir, then leave it to rest for 15 minutes. When it is ready to be used, add 3 eggs and give it a gentle whisk.

— Sieve the buckwheat and the plain flour into a large mixing bowl. Add a generous pinch of nutmeg, and mix together. Form a well in the middle of the flour mixture and pour in the yeasty milk and the water, beer or root beer. Combine the liquids and flours, cover the bowl with a tea towel or clingfilm and leave it to rest for an hour.

— Put a generous glug of sunflower oil into a small non-stick pan followed by a large knob of butter. When the butter has melted, swill the oils around the pan, then pour them out into a small bowl. These oils need to swilled around the frying pan between each pancake, so that the pan always has a thin coating of grease.

— Pour enough of the thick batter into the pan to cover the bottom with a layer about 2-3mm thick. Fry the pancake for a couple of minutes, until the underside is brown, then turn it over with a wide spatula. Fry the second side for a minute or two, then remove the pancake, put it on a plate and cover with tinfoil.

— When you have cooked all the dough, put the plate of pancakes in a warm oven (150°C) for 5-10 minutes to heat through.

When you set aside the batter, you can soak half a bowl of sultanas or raisins in sufficient water or tea to cover them. A small glass of rum or cognac can be added to pep them up. Sprinkle over the pancakes when they are frying in the pan.

A layer of stewed apples, brown sugar and lemon juice can be spread between each pancake, then the pile reheated in the oven at 180°C for 10 minutes and cut into pieces like a cake. Alternatively the pancakes are delicious plain, rolled up with a brown sugar and lemon juice filling, or speculoos paste [→ see recipe p.213].

Liège
SUGAR WAFFLES

10-12 waffles

1 waffle iron

1 large mixing bowl

1 small bowl

Greaseproof paper

1 baking tray

Preparation: 30 minutes

Rising: 75 minutes

Cooking: 30-45 minutes

300g flour

180g soft butter

150g pearl sugar

100g brown sugar

2 large eggs

25g fresh yeast

120ml milk

4 drops vanilla essence

1 large pinch of salt

OPTIONAL:

½ tsp cinnamon

Spray-on cooking oil

1 bar of chocolate

— Wake the fresh yeast up by crumbling it into the warm milk with the vanilla essence. Give it a stir, then leave to rest for 15 minutes.

— In a large mixing bowl, stir together the flour, brown sugar, salt and cinnamon (if it is to your taste) and make a well in the middle to accommodate the lightly beaten eggs and yeasty milk. Stir well, then cover with clingfilm or a tea towel and place somewhere warm for an hour. During this time the dough will double in size.

— Mix the soft butter and pearl sugar into the risen dough. This will knock the gases out of it, making it more elastic.

— Divide the dough into balls the size of generous scoops of ice cream and lay on greaseproof paper on a baking tray. The balls should be at least 3 fingers apart as they need to rest and rise for a further 15 minutes. During this time the waffle iron can come up to temperature. Before you cook the waffles, grease the iron with a squirt of spray-on cooking oil or with a kitchen oil brush.

— Place a ball of dough in the waffle iron and close. It will cook in about 3 minutes and shouldn't be opened during the first minute as the waffle will split.

— When the waffles come out they will be too hot to eat as the sugar will have melted into liquid caramel, but they aren't too hot to push a piece of chocolate into their hot middles, where it will melt and increase the rich delight of this treat.

ⓘ Waffles can be kept in an airtight box for up to a week.

ⓘ If pearl sugar is not available, a good substitute is sugar cubes that have been broken up in a nut grinder or wrapped in a tea towel and given a few blows with a rolling pin.

ⓘ If you don't have a waffle iron, the dough from this recipe can be baked as a cake, called a Verviers Cake. Instead of cutting the dough into waffle-sized pieces, put it into a baking tin (approximately 25cm in diameter) and leave to rise in a warm place for 30 minutes before baking in the middle of an oven at 200°C for 30 minutes.

Fruitful Belgium

EVERY APRIL, BELGIUM'S HASPENGOUW REGION TURNS INTO A MASS OF pink and white flowers as the fruit orchards start to blossom. It's a stunning sight to behold as the apple, pear and cherry trees awaken from their winter slumber and burst into colour.

Haspengouw, a region in the east of the country that criss-crosses several provinces, is Belgium's major fruit-producing area and, according to the local tourist office, is the second-largest fruit region in the whole of Europe. Fruit picked in the region is sold both at home and in the export market. In fact, local fruit was already being exported to England and Germany back in the 19th century.

Today much of the fruit is sold via cooperative fruit auctions, the largest of which is the Belgische Fruitveiling (BFV), or Belgian Fruit Auction. More than 1,500 fruit growers sell their produce via this cooperative, giving it a 50% market share.

Among the varieties of apple found in Belgian orchards are Jonagold, Boskoop and Braeburn. As for pears, the Conference, Doyenné du Comice and Durondeau varieties are among those cultivated here. To give you an idea of volumes, approximately 200 million pears and a similar number of apples are grown every year in Belgium.

So what do the Belgians like to do with all their fruit? As well as eating them raw, they also turn them into fruit juices, jams

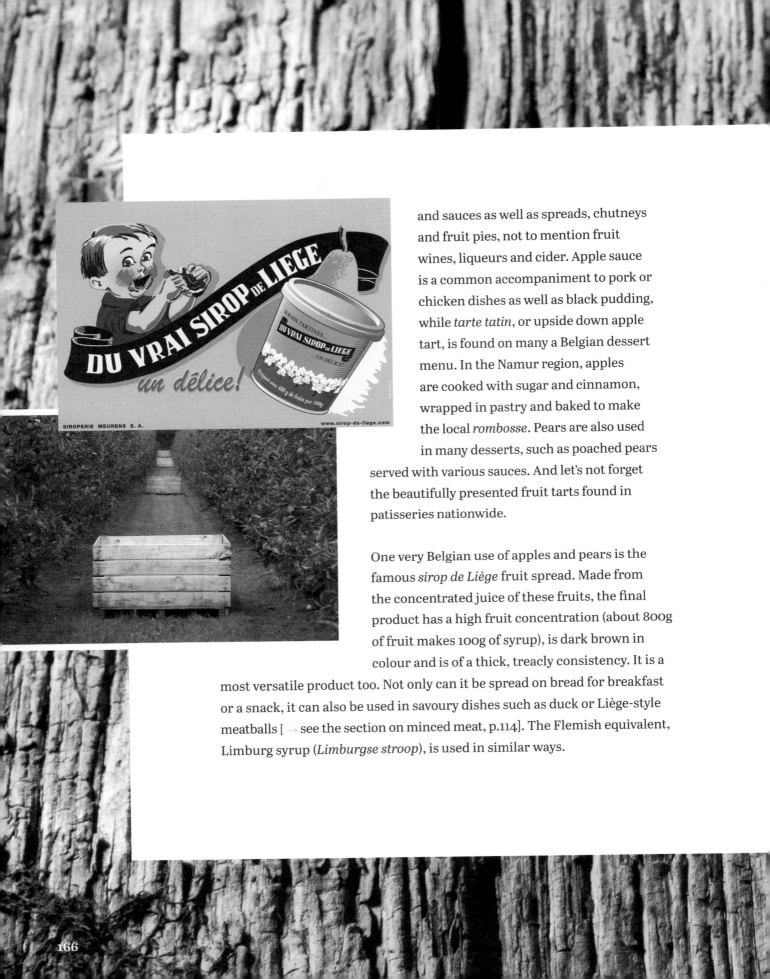

and sauces as well as spreads, chutneys and fruit pies, not to mention fruit wines, liqueurs and cider. Apple sauce is a common accompaniment to pork or chicken dishes as well as black pudding, while *tarte tatin*, or upside down apple tart, is found on many a Belgian dessert menu. In the Namur region, apples are cooked with sugar and cinnamon, wrapped in pastry and baked to make the local *rombosse*. Pears are also used in many desserts, such as poached pears served with various sauces. And let's not forget the beautifully presented fruit tarts found in patisseries nationwide.

One very Belgian use of apples and pears is the famous *sirop de Liège* fruit spread. Made from the concentrated juice of these fruits, the final product has a high fruit concentration (about 800g of fruit makes 100g of syrup), is dark brown in colour and is of a thick, treacly consistency. It is a most versatile product too. Not only can it be spread on bread for breakfast or a snack, it can also be used in savoury dishes such as duck or Liège-style meatballs [→ see the section on minced meat, p.114]. The Flemish equivalent, Limburg syrup (*Limburgse stroop*), is used in similar ways.

CHERRIES AND BERRIES

Cherries are a Belgian staple, with the harvest starting in mid-June and usually lasting until the end of July. As well as being a popular snack on their own, cherries are also served with meatballs and used to make soup, either with sweet or sour *kriek* cherries. This fruit is also an ingredient in the beers known as *krieks* [→ see p. 72 for more about Belgian beers].

Among red fruits, strawberries are probably the most popular, with a major centre being Wépion, a Walloon town south of Namur. The Wépion auction is where many professionals buy their fresh strawberries, and demonstrations are organised for visitors to give them an insight into this world. Wépion even has a strawberry museum, full of pictures, books and objects relating to the fruit's history in the area.

There are plenty of other activities organised in the fruit-growing parts of the country too. On the museum front, there's the Fruit Region Museum (Fruitstreekmusem) in Borgloon, where the spotlight is thrown on the cultivation and processing of fruit as well as the history of the Haspengouw region. In Sint-Truiden there's a blossom ordination in church at the start of the season, while visits to fruit farms and fruit auctions are available in many towns and villages, as are walks, cycles and bus tours around the orchards.

Poached
PEARS

4 servings

1 saucepan

1 casserole dish

1 hour

4 sweet ripe pears

4 tsp sugar

Lemon juice

1 generous pinch of lemon
and orange zest per pear

1 generous pinch of cinnamon
per pear

2 cloves

8 tsp *sirop de Liège*

OPTIONAL:

150 ml apple juice
(if *sirop de Liège* is unavailable)

1 pinch of ginger per pear

1 pinch of pepper per pear

1 tsp cornflour

Pèkèt or brandy

—— Wash and peel the sweet ripe pears, making sure not to remove the stems and place them in a saucepan. Fill the pan with boiling water up to the middle of the pears. Flavour the water with the citrus zest and lemon juice as well as the cinnamon, cloves, and, if they are to your taste, the ginger and pepper.

—— Cover and simmer for half an hour before adding 4 teaspoons of sugar and the *sirop de Liège*. Simmer for a further 15 minutes in an uncovered pan before removing the pears and putting them in a warm casserole dish covered in tinfoil.

—— The sauce must now be thickened. The quick and easy way is to mix 1 teaspoon of cornflour to a quarter of a cup of cold water and add it to the sauce. (But this is pejoratively nicknamed the wallpaper paste solution.) More effective is to increase the heat under the poaching liquid for 10-15 minutes in order for it to reduce. A few drops of brandy, kirsch, Poire Williams or *pèkèt* can be added to the sauce to perk it up.

—— Place the pears in dessert bowls and pour over the warm sauce.

The ripeness of a pear can be checked by pressing on the stalk end: unripe pears are hard whilst ripe ones yield.

This dish is frequently accompanied by ice cream, whipped cream, chocolate sauce and dry-roasted almonds. Served cold, it can be accompanied by rice pudding, redcurrants, fruit salad and a few mint leaves.

Some pears stand out as having the right flavour and texture for stewing. Most suitable is the St Remy, but also highly rated are the Conference, Doyenne de Comice, Bons Chretiens, Anjou, Seckel, Emile d'Heyst, Packham's Triumph, Winter Nelis, Pitmaston Duchess and Legipont.

If *sirop de Liège* is unavailable, replace half the boiling water with apple juice.

CHERRY
tart

1 tart (6-8 servings)

1 pie tin (± 23cm)
Greaseproof paper
Baking beans
2 bowls

Preparation: 40 minutes
Cooking: 35-40 minutes

FOR THE PASTRY:
Home-made shortcrust pastry
[→ see p.179]
(or shop-bought pre-rolled
pastry)

FOR THE FILLING:
350g pitted cherries
150g sugar
3 eggs
100g self-raising flour
(or plain flour and 1tsp of
baking powder)
1 tsp cinnamon

— Wash and pit the cherries. A cherry pitter will make this job fast and easy, but if you don't have one, use the side of the blade of a large, wide chef's knife to crush the cherries, much like you might a clove of garlic. Alternatively, use a short sharp knife to cut the cherries down the middle and pop the pip out with the point of the knife.

— Roll the dough out to the size of your pie tin, allowing for 4cm of crust on each side. Transfer the dough to the tin and blind bake (cover the base of the dough with a piece of greaseproof paper and put a handful of baking beans on top) for 20 minutes in a preheated oven at 180°C.

— Separate 3 eggs and whisk the yolks until they start to foam. Sieve the self-raising flour into the yolks, and to this, add the sugar and a generous pinch of cinnamon. Mix together until you have a breadcrumb-like consistency. In a separate bowl whisk the whites until they form peaks and then carefully fold into the flour mixture.

— Spread the cherries evenly across the pre-baked pastry and sprinkle a teaspoon of cinnamon over the top. Pour the filling evenly over the cherries and put straight in the oven at 180°C for 35-40 minutes until the topping is golden brown.

ⁱ Serve warm with a kriek beer or a glass of cherry juice.

ⁱ A cherry tart should be made with very ripe cherries, the darker the better. As the cherry season is short, just June and July in Belgium, preserved cherries can be used out of season.

ⁱ If cherries are unavailable then raspberries, blueberries, pears, blackcurrants, redcurrants, gooseberries or rhubarb are all good substitutes.

And for dessert: pies and tarts

BELGIAN DESSERTS COME IN MANY SHAPES AND FORMS, RANGING FROM the traditional homemade pie to exquisite creations sold in the local patisserie. As with so many other Belgian foods, many towns pride themselves on their particular specialty.

The *Geraardsbergse mattentaart* (*tarte au maton* in French) is one that has achieved more fame than most, having been granted the European Union's Protected Geographical Status, a recognition that means the name can only be used for the true *Mattentaart* made in the Geraardsbergen area. The tradition of baking these small tartlets, made from flaky pastry and filled with curd, eggs and almonds, goes back centuries, with a reference even found in a 13th century troubadour song. Today there is a group that keeps the tradition alive and which, among other things, organises an annual *Mattentaart* day on the marketplace in Geraardsbergen. The *mattentaart* was also the first regional product to appear on a postage stamp, in 1985.

As for rice tarts, these are a dessert strongly associated with the town of Verviers in the eastern province of Liège. The people of the town have even established an association (la Seigneurie de la Vervi-Riz) to spread the word of the local rice tart and defend its traditions: the association has a committee whose members wear special robes, there is an oath that members must take, and it has a special 4-line motto:

Jamais pour me nourrir,
Toujours pour le plaisir
Magnans, Frés, fât qu'on rêye, (mangeons, frères, il faut rire)
Avou nosse blanque dorêye (avec notre tarte au riz)
(It's never just for nourishment – It's always for the pleasure – Brothers,
let's eat, for we must laugh – With our rice tart.)

The earliest record of the rice tart is thought to be in a cookery book from 1604 written by Lancelot de Casteau, the master cook of three princes of Liège. At the time, the ingredients of sugar and spices were considered luxuries and so it was most probably a food for the rich, or at the very least one for special occasions. Today, rice tarts and tartlets are found in bakeries nationwide.

Another popular rice-based dessert in Belgium is rice pudding. Belgians revere it to the extent that they have an expression describing heaven as somewhere where you eat rice pudding every day with golden spoons. They quite simply consider it divine.

In Flanders, the locals enjoy their *vlaaien*, which is best translated as pies, although they're somewhere between pies, cakes and flans. In fact, the Flemish have been enjoying them for centuries, as illustrated by a 16th century Pieter Brueghel painting where a roof is tiled with these pies, an image that has found its way into a local expression to indicate a place of plenty. (*Daar zijn de daken met vlaaien bedekt* – There the roofs are tiled with pies.)

A PIE FOR EVERYONE

Different towns have their own particular pies. The Aalst pie for example is made from cinnamon rolls, milk and sugar. It is a pie that has become a real part of Aalst's local heritage, with Myriam Bockstael in 1981 recording the song *De Aalsterse vlaaien* (The Aalst pies), which is now kept in the local archives, and a couple of years later a pie guild being established with its own coat of arms.

In Lier, the pies are made from a recipe that dates back some 300 years, the exact ingredients of which are only known to local bakers. Lier pies are small and round, have a drier texture and darker colour than other pies (as they are not made with eggs) and have a distinct spiciness to their taste.

In the province of Limburg, the land of orchards, the pie for which it is best known is a fruit pie with a lattice pastry on the top. Another dessert from this part of the country has one of the most fun names: Smurf tart (*Smurfentaart*). That said, it is not entirely clear why this particular dessert, made with apricots, whipped cream and white chocolate flakes, is named after the blue Belgian comic figures.

For other fun-named sweet treats, don't overlook Malmedy Kisses (*Baisers de Malmedy*), meringues filled with whipped cream. Malmedy, a small town in the province of Liège, is the place that is best known for its Kisses, but there are also Kisses from Flawinne, Rochefort and other locations.

Then there are a few places in the country that are simply renowned as being cake meccas, for example Chaumont-Gistoux, where Les Tartes de Chaumont-Gistoux was established in 1945 and is still a place to which Belgians flock for that special cake, or Tancrémont, where locals and visitors patiently queue outside Au Vieux Tancrémont to buy one (or more!) of its famous fruit, sugar or rice tarts.

RICE
tart

1 pie (6-8 servings)

1 baking tin (23-26cm)

1 saucepan

1 milk pan

1 mixing bowl

2 small bowls

Preparation: 2 hours

Cooking: 25-35 minutes

FOR THE BRIOCHE DOUGH:

150g flour

10g fresh yeast

75ml milk

50g soft butter

1 egg

1 tbsp sugar

1 pinch of salt

FOR THE FILLING:

1 litre milk (up to half can be

replaced by cream)

150g short grain/pudding rice

150g caster sugar

3 eggs

1 tsp vanilla essence

(or 1 vanilla stick (5cm))

1 pinch of salt

OPTIONAL:

A few threads saffron

50g raisins

1 tsp cinnamon

1 tbsp jam

THE BRIOCHE DOUGH:

— Warm 75ml of milk and crumble the fresh yeast into it with a pinch of sugar. Stir well so that all the yeast dissolves and set aside for 15 minutes. While it is resting, sift the flour into a large mixing bowl. Add sugar and a pinch of salt. Stir together and then make a well in the centre. Lightly beat an egg and pour this and the yeasty milk into the centre of the flour. Bring the dough together and then incorporate the soft butter. Do this only for as long as is necessary to produce a soft and elastic dough – overworking it will produce a tough tart base. Expect the dough to be sticky, but resist the temptation to add more flour. Cover with a damp towel and leave to rise for 60 minutes.

— When the dough has doubled in size, turn it out onto a lightly floured board or work surface, then lift and drop it a few times to knock out the pockets of air. Roll it out to a thickness of about ½cm. The tart base needs to be as wide as your baking tin plus 3-4cm on either side for the crust. Butter the tin, then transfer the rolled dough into it and prick with a fork a dozen times. Cover with a damp towel and allow to rise again for half an hour.

THE FILLING:

— While the dough is rising for the first time, wash the loose starch out of the rice before cooking it in the milk (or milk and cream combination) and sugar, with a pinch of salt and the vanilla essence or fresh vanilla pod. Adding a few strands of saffron to the milk will turn the rice a wonderful golden colour. Cook for 45 minutes to an hour on a very low, simmering heat, until all the liquid has been absorbed. Be careful to stir regularly as the rice can easily burn on the bottom of the pan.

— Once the rice has the consistency of thick porridge, take it off the heat and let it cool. When the rice is no longer steaming when stirred, separate the eggs and mix in the yolks. You can add a teaspoon of cinnamon, a small handful of raisins or other dried fruit. Finally, beat the egg whites until they have a stiff frothy texture and gently fold them in.

— For a sweeter dessert, line the pastry with jam. Then pour in the mixture and cook in the centre of a pre-heated oven at 200°C for 25-35 minutes. Remove when the rice filling turns a mottled brown and golden-yellow colour.

SUGAR
tart

1 tart (6-8 servings)

1 large mixing bowl

1 small mixing bowl

1 baking tin (23-26cm)

Greaseproof paper

Baking beans

Preparation: 30 minutes

Refrigeration:

20 minutes

Cooking: 40 minutes

FOR THE SHORTCRUST
PASTRY:

150g plain flour

2 tbsp sugar

1 egg

75g butter

2 tbsp cold water

1 pinch of salt

FOR THE FILLING:

50g butter

100g brown sugar

100g caster sugar

50ml cream

2 egg yolks

40g ground almonds

(or hazelnuts)

1 tsp vanilla essence

THE SHORTCRUST PASTRY:

— Mix the butter with the sieved flour, sugar and a pinch of salt until they take on a fine breadcrumb consistency. The most rapid and efficient way to do this is to give the ingredients a 15-20 second blast in a blender.

— Make a well in the middle of the dough and add the lightly beaten egg and a couple of tablespoons of cold water. Using your fingers, bring the mixture together until the liquid is absorbed and you have a ball of flexible dough. If it sticks to your fingers, add a pinch more flour. Wrap the dough in clingfilm and put it in the fridge for 20 minutes.

— Remove the pastry from the clingfilm and place on a board with a very light dusting of flour. Roll it out with a floured rolling pin, exerting firm pressure and turning the dough 90° after each roll. If cracks appear in the pastry, push it back together by hand. Roll it to the diameter of your baking tin, adding a generous 3cm crust on each side.

— Transfer the dough to the baking tin and blind bake (cover the base of the dough with a piece of greaseproof paper and put a handful of baking beans on top) for 20 minutes in a preheated oven at 180°C. Once cooked, the pastry should be dry and light brown in colour.

THE FILLING:

— Cut 50g of butter into 6 sugar cube sized pieces and chill them in a freezer for 15 minutes or the fridge for an hour: they need to be hard.

— Mix the brown sugar, white sugar and ground nuts, and spread this evenly over the base. Space the fridge-chilled dices of butter evenly on top and lightly beat 2 egg yolks with the cream and a teaspoon of vanilla essence before pouring over the sugar.

— Place in the centre of a pre-heated oven at 200°C for 20 minutes, until the filling has caramelised.

i This sweet tart is traditionally made with a yeast-risen brioche dough base [→ see recipe on p.176] but you can also use shortcrust pastry as explained above, or store-bought pre-rolled pastry dough.

i A sugar tart is best served cool or lukewarm, with fresh berries, sliced peaches or melon.

In the biscuit jar

NAME A BELGIAN TOWN AND MORE OFTEN THAN NOT IT'LL HAVE A biscuit for which it is well known: Antwerp has its *handjes* (little hands), Bruges its *kletskoppen* (flat heads or chatterboxes) and Dinant its *couques*, or cookies. And behind every biscuit there always seems to be an intriguing story.

Take the *couques de Dinant*, whose origins are said to go back to the middle of the 15th century when the town was under siege by Charles the Bold. Having little in the way of provisions, the citizens of Dinant used what they had: honey and flour. Mixed together into a paste, placed in finely worked copper moulds and then baked in the oven, the result was a hard, honey-flavoured biscuit. With their designs of flowers, grapes or town views, these biscuits are still found throughout the town today. A word of warning before eating them: they should be sucked or dunked into tea or coffee, not bitten. They're so hard that if you tried to bite them, you'd probably break your teeth.

The use of moulds is also part and parcel of what is arguably Belgium's most famous biscuit: *speculoos*, a light brown, crunchy biscuit with a flavour of ginger, cinnamon and other spices. Traditionally made for Saint Nicholas's Day (December 6), a festive day in Belgium when children receive presents, the biscuits often have an image of the saint imprinted on them. Some of the large old wooden moulds can be seen at the Belgian biscuit maker Dandoy, whose flagship store is just off the Grand' Place (central square) in Brussels.

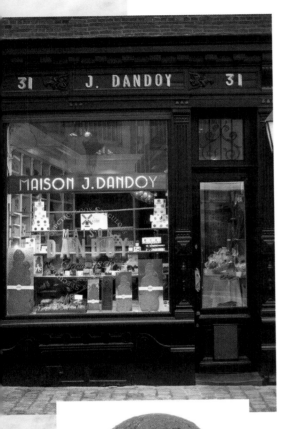

These days speculoos is not just served in December, but is a common companion to a cup of coffee in a Belgian café all year round. The traditional biscuit has also adapted to evolving culinary tastes, being served as an accompaniment to savoury foods such as foie gras or crumbled into a powder and sprinkled on dishes. It can also be found as an ice-cream flavour and in jars of speculoos paste, which now sell in their millions and are exported far and wide.

Spices are used in other Belgian biscuits too, for example the almond thins made famous by Jules Destrooper. Destrooper, a colonial trader, founded his biscuit company in 1886, flavouring his products with the spices he had discovered and then imported from Africa and the East.

Another well-known name in the world of Belgian biscuit makers is Delacre, which before it started making biscuits at the end of the 19th century was a chocolate manufacturer. Delacre claims to be the first to have combined a biscuit with pure Belgian chocolate.

THE CLÉMENT CONNECTION

Many of the country's well-known biscuits can be found in the Belgian gastronomic reference book *Le Conseiller Culinaire*, written by chef Gaston Clément, including *bernardins* from the province of Hainault, *mokken* from Ghent and Brussels' *pain à la Grecque*.

Bernardins are oval-shaped almond biscuits, light brown in colour with an almond on top resembling a monk's habit and white belt. According to one version of history, the Bernardin monks passed down the recipe to a biscuit maker in Chimay. Another town in the same province is also home to a Bernardin biscuit – Fleurus, or to give it its nickname *Cité des Bernardins*. Ghent's *mokken* have been enjoyed in the Flemish town for centuries and are said to have been a favourite of the Holy Roman Emperor Charles V, who was born there. They resemble macaroons with a cinnamon and aniseed flavour. As for *pain à la Grecque*, don't be fooled by its name, which literally means Greek-style bread. In fact, this bread-like biscuit comes from Brussels. In times gone by there used to be an Augustine church in the city centre and the monks would give bread to the poor in the nearby street, Wolvengracht. The bread therefore became known as 'bread from the *gracht*' and over time the word '*gracht*' turned into 'Greek'.

The *kletskoppen* of Bruges gain their name, according to Gaston Clément, from the almonds and hazelnuts in the recipe that resemble little heads (*koppen*); others say it is because the dough is placed on the baking tray like little round heads that are then flattened (*kletsen*) to make these wafer thin biscuits; yet others say they owe their origin to the word's meaning of 'chatterbox' because the biscuits would be eaten with tea or coffee and a chat. The French name for the biscuits is much simpler: *dentelles de Bruges* (Bruges lace), referring to their lace-like appearance.

As for Antwerp's *handjes*, these take their name from the story of the giant Druoon Antigoon. According to legend, the giant demanded a very high toll from the ships that passed by Antwerp on the river Scheldt, and those who refused to pay had a hand chopped off. Silvius Brabo challenged the giant to a fight, killed him and threw one of the giant's hands in the river. Today not only is there a biscuit to recall the story, but a statue of Brabo holding a chopped-off hand in the central market square.

Bruges
KLETSKOPPEN

🍴 30 biscuits

🔪 1 small mixing bowl

1 non-stick baking tray

🕐 Preparing: 15 minutes

Refrigeration: 1 hour

Cooking: 10 minutes

45g flour

90g brown sugar

45g soft butter

25g sliced almonds

1 pinch of salt

2 drops of vanilla essence

1 drop of almond essence

1 tbsp water or orange juice

OPTIONAL:

1 pinch of grated orange zest

1 pinch of cinnamon

— Mix the sugar, soft butter, 1 tablespoon of water or orange juice, the drops of vanilla and almond essence and a pinch of salt, then sieve in the flour and add the almonds and orange zest or cinnamon if they are to your taste. When the mix is smooth, wrap the dough in clingfilm and put in the fridge for at least an hour, but ideally overnight.

— When the dough has hardened, transfer it to a non-stick baking tray a small ball at a time. Leave at least 10cm between each mound of mix. Press each ball down on them with the palm of your hand to flatten then to a thickness of just a few millimetres. There should be 3 or 4 fingers-width separating the biscuits now.

— Cooking requires close supervision to ensure that the biscuits don't burn. Cooking times will vary from oven to oven, but in general they need about 8 minutes in a pre-heated oven at 180°C.

— When the biscuits are hazelnut brown, transfer them to a plate to cool.

ⓘ Kletskoppen are very sweet, making them an excellent accompaniment for ice cream and other desserts.

ⓘ Kletskoppen dough keeps in the fridge for up to a week, or can be frozen for up to 3 months. As the biscuits come out of the oven, you might want to wrap them round the handle of a wooden spoon to give them a cigar shape, bend them into a bowl shape, or twist them into other unusual shapes.

Classic
SPECULOOS

🍴 40-50 biscuits

🔪 2 mixing bowls

1 baking tray

Greaseproof paper

🕐 Preparation: 30 minutes

Refrigeration: overnight

Cooking: 15-20 minutes

500g plain

(or self-raising flour)

300g brown sugar

1 egg

100 ml milk (or water)

150g soft unsalted butter

3 tsp cinnamon

½ tsp finely ground pepper

½ tsp finely ground cloves

½ tsp finely ground nutmeg

½ tsp ground cardamom

1 tsp ground dried ginger

1 tsp finely ground star anise

1 pinch of salt

OPTIONAL:

75g ground almonds

1 tsp baking powder (if you are

using plain flour)

—— Sieve the flour into a mixing bowl and stir in the spices, a pinch of salt, and the ground almonds if you choose to use them. In another mixing bowl, lightly beat an egg and then mix in the sugar, soft butter and milk or water. This is much more easily done using an electric mixer than by hand. Combine the contents of the 2 bowls to produce a smooth yet heavy dough. If it is hard to mix the ingredients, add a splash of cold water.

—— The dough must now be refrigerated for several hours (ideally overnight) in a Tupperware or a bowl covered in clingfilm.

—— Roll the dough out on a lightly floured surface. When it is about ½cm thick, use a cookie cutter or knife to cut into rectangles or ovals and place a thumb width apart on a baking tray lined with greaseproof paper.

—— Place in the middle of a preheated oven at 170°C for 15-20 minutes. Remove when they start turning from a light golden to a dark hazelnut colour. After 10 minutes' cooking time the biscuits need to be watched closely: their high sugar content means that they burn quickly.

—— When ready, remove from the tray and cool on a wire rack. Stored in an airtight box, speculoos will keep for several weeks.

ⓘ Packets of pre-mixed speculoos spice are available at most Belgian markets and supermarkets.

ⓘ Don't be put off if some of the spices on this list are missing in your kitchen: the ones you can't do without are cinnamon and cloves.

ⓘ If you would like to bake these biscuits in smaller batches, speculoos dough freezes well for up to 2 months.

Chocolate, the nation's pride and joy

I F THERE'S ONE FOOD THAT IS SYNONYMOUS WITH BELGIUM THEN IT HAS TO be chocolate. This is the land of pralines, high-quality chocolate bars and arguably the tastiest chocolate desserts you have ever tried.

The history of chocolate in this part of the world stretches back to the 16th century when the Spanish conquistadors discovered the cocoa bean in Mexico and then brought it to the Spanish Netherlands (a geographical area that included present-day Belgium). At that time chocolate was still very much considered a luxury and was mainly consumed as a drink. It was not until the industrialisation of production methods and the introduction of cocoa plantations in the African colonies in the 19th century that chocolate became available to a much wider population and was used much more diversely.

As colonial ruler in the Congo, Belgium had an unlimited supply of cocoa from the plantations there: this is why it is sometimes said that the history of Belgian chocolate is not all sweet. Another advantage that Belgium had was its coal industry, which meant it had the technology needed for grinding the beans.

It is in the last 100 years, however, that Belgium has cemented its reputation as a chocolate capital. One major milestone was the creation of the praline in 1912 by Jean Neuhaus, whose grandfather had arrived in Belgium from Switzerland in the late 1850s and opened a shop in Brussels' Galerie de la Reine selling cough sweets, liquorice and bars of bitter chocolate. When Jean took over the business, it didn't take him long to create the praline, and as a result Neuhaus is today a world-famous chocolate house.

Another landmark in the development of Belgium's chocolate history was the 1958 World Expo in Brussels, which included a pavilion where the latest chocolate recipes were presented to the world. Côte d'Or, already renowned for its Chokotoffs (chocolate toffee sweets) and its Mignonettes (small squares of chocolate) both of which remain popular today, presented its Dessert 58 at the Expo. The chocolate company described its new creation as 'a unique praline recipe made with almonds and hazelnuts, specially created for the occasion'.

Today, Belgium is home to more than 250 chocolate and praline companies, generating more than 4 billion euros in sales, according to the Royal Belgian Association of the Biscuit, Chocolate, Pralines and Confectionary Industries.

PRALINES AND SO ON

Walk down any shopping street, be it in Brussels, Bruges or Binche, and you'll be sure to find one of the big praline makers such as Neuhaus, Godiva or Leonidas. Stroll around the Sablon area of Brussels and as well as the antiques shops you'll also find upmarket chocolatiers. On one corner there is Pierre Marcolini, whose window display resembles that of an art and design shop with its exquisite chocolate creations, while in the centre there is Wittamer, Official Supplier to the Court of Belgium, and further up there is Passion Chocolat, which prides itself on its innovative creations.

The different types of pralines and truffles are too numerous to list, but one worth a special mention is the Charleroi *gayette*. In 1987 a sweet shop in Charleroi, a former coal-mining region, asked the chocolate maker Gilbert Blancke to create a local product. He came up with a small black truffle that looked like a piece of coal and called it *gayette*, a Walloon word meaning a small piece of coal given to miners to keep warm. In this way, chocolate has helped to keep the region's history alive.

Chocolate also plays an important role on any Belgian dessert menu. There you'll be sure to find *Dame Blanche*, literally 'white lady', which is simply vanilla ice cream with dark melted chocolate poured on top. The quality of the chocolate ensures that it tastes heavenly. Another favourite on the dessert menu is a *moelleux au chocolat*, which roughly translates as chocolate fondant. The moelleux is like the croquette of the dessert world: crispy on the outside and smooth and creamy on the inside. Then of course there is chocolate mousse and the chocolate bomb, which is like a refrigerated mousse covered in cocoa powder.

Nor must chocolate spread be forgotten, served on bread as a favourite with children for an afternoon snack as well as on the brunch table on Sundays. Or chocolate as a filling in a waffle or pancake. The possibilities are almost limitless. In fact in 2013 the Belgian post office even issued stamps that smelled and tasted of chocolate!

CHOCOLATE
mousse

4 servings

1 bain-marie
(heatproof bowl resting
on a saucepan)

1 mixing bowl

4 glasses or ramekins
for serving

Preparation: 40 minutes

Refrigeration: 2-4 hours

250g chocolate

200ml chilled double cream

4 eggs

60g superfine caster sugar

2 tbsp water (or coffee)

1 pinch of sea salt

OPTIONAL:

2 drops lemon juice

40 g unsalted butter

— Melt 250g of roughly chopped chocolate mixed with 2 tablespoons of water or coffee in a bain-marie or a microwave on a low power setting. Stir the chocolate occasionally so that it doesn't boil or burn. As soon as the chocolate turns liquid, remove from the heat. Adding a pinch of sea salt will open up its flavour. If the chocolate is bitter and your taste is for gentler flavours then you should add a knob of butter.

— Whip the chilled cream until it is as thick as yoghurt and the whisk leaves a trail on its surface. Separate the eggs and vigorously whisk the yolks into the melted chocolate, using an electric whisk. After a minute, add the sugar and whipped cream and repeat the energetic whisking for a couple more minutes.

— Whisk the egg whites to a firm foam. Adding a couple of drops of lemon juice will make this quicker. Stop whisking as soon as the foam forms peaks when you lift the whisk: over-beaten whites will collapse back into a runny liquid.

— Fold the frothy egg whites into the chocolate a third at a time. When the mousse has an even consistency, spoon into martini glasses, ramekin dishes or a larger serving bowl and chill in the fridge for 2-4 hours until it has set.

ⓘ A good mousse begins with good chocolate: Belgian is best! Some people will shy away from the intense, bitter flavour of chocolate with a high cocoa content, preferring a lighter, sweeter milk chocolate. This recipe can be made with either or, even better, both.

ⓘ When serving the mousse, you can bring out a fresher note by combining it with kiwi, strawberry, raspberry, tamarind, apple, passion fruit purée, papaya, mint, candied fennel or green tea. Alternatively the spicier notes can be accentuated by accompanying the mousse with coffee, almond liqueur, mulled wine, cherry eau-de-vie, cointreau, candied orange peel, orange segments, marmalade, blackcurrants, black pepper, red hot chillis, dried cranberries, rhubarb, figs, roasted almonds, crystallized ginger or cinnamon.

Chocolate
MOELLEUX

4 servings

1 bain-marie
(heatproof bowl resting
on a saucepan)
2 mixing bowls
4 ramekins
(or silicon moulds)

30 minutes

150g bitter black chocolate
(+70% cocoa content)
150g soft unsalted butter
2 eggs
2 egg yolks
100g sugar
70g flour
1 pinch of salt

— Turn the oven to 220°C and then melt the chocolate and butter in a bain-marie or a microwave on a low power setting, stirring occasionally. Make sure that the bottom of the bowl is not touching the water.

— While the chocolate and butter are melting, whisk 2 eggs and 2 egg yolks with 100g of sugar using an electric whisk for 2-3 minutes until the mixture has the consistency of melted vanilla ice cream.

— When the chocolate and butter have melted, take the bowl off the heat and sieve in 70g of plain flour, stirring as you go. Add a pinch of salt, then mix in the sweet eggs. Pour the mixture into 4 greased ramekins or silicon moulds, and cook in the oven for 10-12 minutes at 220°C.

— The moelleux will rise a little and harden around their edges. They are ready when they are still soft and a little runny in the middle. Remove them from the ramekin dishes 5 minutes after taking them out of the oven.

Moelleux can be served warm or cold, alone or accompanied by baked figs, red fruits, custard, ice cream and/or salted caramel sauce.

The spirit of Belgium

THE TIPPLE OF PREFERENCE IN BELGIUM IS GENEVER, OR *PÈKÈT* AS THE Francophones call this distilled spirit. One Flemish town with a strong genever tradition is Hasselt, home to the National Genever Museum, an annual genever festival and a fountain that spouts the spirit. In the south of the country, annual festivities in Liège, Namur and many other Walloon towns would not be complete without their trays of brightly coloured, fruit-flavoured pèkèt shots.

The name genever derives from the Dutch word for juniper (*jenever*), the berry used to flavour the grain-based spirit. Consumed in this part of the world since the Middle Ages when it was used for medicinal purposes, genever is today an EU-protected product, meaning that it can only be made in Belgium, the Netherlands and a couple of nearby areas. In this way the spirit enjoys a similar status to cognac or Scotch whisky in their respective regions.

For Koen De Jans, owner of the Stokerij Wissels distillery in Hasselt, a good genever can rival a single malt whisky. For him, it is a spirit with a refined taste that must be savoured. His distillery prides itself on making genever from pure malt, using traditional techniques and old-fashioned copper stills.

Drinking genever has undergone highs and lows in Belgium during the last century, predominantly due to the Vandervelde law, which came into effect in 1918 and introduced tight restrictions on the sale of distilled spirits. The law, which remained in place until 1983, is considered to be one of the reasons why Belgian beers are so strong, as the people turned to beer instead of spirits.

One bar that opened shortly after the legislation was relaxed in the 1980s is De Vagant, in Antwerp, which aimed – and still aims today – to highlight Belgium's rich genever heritage. As well as being drunk neat, genever is also a popular ingredient in Belgian cocktails. The signature 'De Vagant' cocktail is a killer combination of young genever, lemon genever, fruit juice, Triple Sec and Mandarine Napoléon.

Mandarine Napoléon, a liqueur made from cognac, mandarin orange peel, herbs and spices, is a Belgian specialty distilled at Biercée distillery in the south of the country. The original idea of macerating mandarins in alcohol and blending the distillate with cognac was that of Napoléon's doctor Antoine-François de Fourcroy, and the drink is said to have been a favourite of Napoléon, whose empire at the time stretched into present-day Belgium. During the 19th century a Belgian chemist, Louis Schmidt, discovered the recipe in Fourcroy's diary and decided to create a liqueur from it. The first bottle of Mandarine Napoléon appeared in 1892.

A much more recent addition to the country's range of strong drinks is whisky. It was the dream of distiller Etienne Bouillon to create a company dedicated to making single malts in Belgium, and that dream became reality in 2004 when the first cask of Belgian Single Malt Whisky was filled. Located in Grâce-Hollogne, just outside Liège, the Owl Distillery uses barley grown in the Hesbaye region and prides itself on a product that has gone on to win many awards.

ELIXIRS

Another group of popular drinks in Belgium are elixirs, for example *Elixir d'Anvers* (Antwerp elixir), a liqueur prepared from more than 30 plants and herbs. The benefits of this elixir, other than simple enjoyment, are said to include being a remedy against stomach ache, abdominal pain and even colic in horses. The drink has received numerous awards, including one in 1887 that was signed by Louis Pasteur.

There's also the *Elixir de Spa*, distilled by the friars of the Capuchin Order near Spa as far back as the 12th century. In nearby Franchimont, several local drinks make a special appearance at the town's famous medieval festival organised every other year, for example the *Fleur de Franchimont*, a fermented apple drink that is mixed with local wild flowers and is said to have antioxidant qualities.

Heading further south towards Luxembourg is the Belgian town of Arlon whose traditional drink is an aperitif called *Maitrank*, or literally 'May drink'. While the alcoholic content comes from white wine and sometimes cognac, the aperitif's key ingredient is woodruff, a white-flowered plant that abounds in the region's beech woods in spring. The drink is served cold with a slice of orange.

As well as being enjoyed as drinks, these spirits have also found their way into local cuisine, with a splash of *Maitrank* or *Elixir de Spa* being added to sauces or marinades and *Fleur de Franchimont* part of a local raspberry dessert. The spirits are also used to flavour sweet treats such as sorbets and pralines.

Belgian
COCKTAILS

1 bottle (250ml) white beer

100ml lemon genever

2 slices of lemon

PITTIG WITTEKE

— *Pittig witteke* means something like 'spicy little white beer drink'. Pour a bottle of white wheat beer (such as Hoegaarden, Blanche de Namur or Watou's Wit) into a tall glass followed by half a wine glass of lemon genever and two slices of lemon.

(Courtesy of *Ons kookboek*)

40ml Tanqueray Ten gin

20ml brown beer syrup (see instructions below)

20ml Biercée cherry liqueur

10ml fresh lemon juice

Champagne or prosecco

SCARLET DREAMS

Pour the gin, brown beer syrup, cherry liqueur and fresh lemon juice into a cocktail shaker and shake well. Pour into a coupette glass and top up with brut champagne or prosecco.

(Courtesy of Ghent bartender Kristof Burm)

To make 180ml of the beer syrup (suitable for 9 cocktails), pour a bottle of brown beer (250ml; 6-12% ABV) into a saucepan with 30g of sugar and heat for about 5 minutes, until the sugar has dissolved and a quarter of the volume of the beer has evaporated.

60ml *pèkèt* (or genever)

60ml passion-fruit juice

60ml orange juice

½ passion fruit

60ml sparkling water

BLANC PASSION

Pour the *pèkèt*, passion-fruit juice and orange juice into a shaker with a small amount of crushed ice and the flesh of half a fresh passion fruit. Fill a quarter of a tall glass with the sparkling water and top up with the alcoholic juice.

120ml Mandarine Napoléon

60ml fresh lemon juice

1 orange slice

1 cucumber slice

1 raspberry

1 strawberry

Champagne or prosecco

THE PISCINE

Fill a large wine glass with ice and pour in the Mandarine Napoléon, lemon juice and fruits, and stir. Top up with champagne or prosecco.

Alcoholic
COFFEES

1 shot of genever

1 cup of coffee

Cream

HASSELT COFFEE

— This is the Flemish equivalent of an Irish coffee, with the whiskey replaced by genever. Pour the genever into a heat-resistant glass and then fill almost to the top with coffee and stir. Add a layer of cream, gently pouring it over the back of a spoon so that it floats on top of the fortified coffee.

1 shot of *pèkèt*

1 cup of espresso coffee

2 scoops of mocha ice cream

Whipped cream

Cocoa powder

LIÈGE COFFEE

— Pour a measure of *pèkèt* (the genever of Wallonia) into a cup of espresso coffee and stir. Put two scoops of mocha ice cream into a heat-resistant glass and pour the fortified coffee over them. Top with whipped cream and sprinkle with cocoa powder.

1/3 glass of Mandarine Napoléon

1 cup of coffee

Cream

MANDARINE NAPOLÉON COFFEE

— In a heat-resistant glass, fill ⅓ with Mandarine Napoléon and then fill to a centimetre of the top with coffee. Stir, and if you like it piping hot, give it a short blast in the microwave. Add a layer of cream, gently pouring it over the back of a spoon so that it floats on top of the fortified coffee.

1 shot of *advocaat* liqueur

1 cup of coffee

COFFEE AND ADVOCAAT

— In Flanders, coffee is often served with a small glass of *advocaat* liqueur, which is similar to eggnog. This can be consumed separately with a spoon or added to the coffee.

Homemade
ADVOCAAT

 About 1 litre

🕐 15 minutes

8 egg yolks

400g caster sugar

The seeds of 1 vanilla pod
(or 2 packets of vanilla sugar)

500ml full-fat cream

250ml strong alcohol

— Beat the egg yolks with the vanilla and sugar until the sugar is completely dissolved and the mixture is white and frothy.

— Lightly whip the cream into a soft foam and then stir it into the sweet egg mixture.

— Whisk in the alcohol drop by drop, and when it is all mixed in, pour the custard-like mixture into clean glass jars. Seal the jars and store in the fridge.

ℹ To make this recipe, you should use the strongest alcohol you can find. The best option is a clear spirit with an alcohol content of between 80° and 96°, the kind sold in supermarkets for making eau-de-vie. However a good *advocaat* can also be made with brandy, cognac or a strong plain genever.

ℹ *Advocaat* will keep for several months and is at its best when it is at least a week old.

ℹ As well as being a fine complement to coffee, *advocaat* can also accompany ice cream or pancakes.

Special occasions

CHRISTMAS COMES EARLY IN BELGIUM, WITH THE FIRST PRESENTS OF the season arriving on December 6, Saint Nicholas's day. It is a day when children are showered with sweet treats such as marzipan, gingerbread biscuits (*speculoos*) and chocolate, often in the shape of the bishop Saint Nicholas (*Sinterklaas* in Dutch, *Saint Nicolas* in French) or other festive figures.

Saint Nicholas's day marks the start of the festive season and the time Belgians start thinking about what they will cook for one of the most important family meals of the year: Christmas dinner. Unlike in the United Kingdom where turkey is the centrepiece of a traditional Christmas meal, in Belgium there are no rules other than it must be something special.

The Christmas main course could be turkey, but it could just as easily be game, duck or goose. Salmon or shellfish are also popular choices, although these are often eaten as a starter. A platter of special cheeses is par for the course, and as far as desserts go, a traditional choice is the Yule log, a cream cake in the shape of a wooden log. Ice cream dishes are also popular and often sold in the shape of a Yule log too. It goes without saying that chocolate, pralines, biscuits and marzipan sweets are all musts in a Belgian household at this time of year. Sweet raisin bread in the shape of a swaddled baby Jesus, and known as *cougnou* or baby Jesus bread, is also traditionally baked during this period.

The festive season is marked in many Belgian towns by a Christmas market, with a giant Christmas tree in the central square around which there are wooden huts

selling all sorts of gifts, food and drink. The smell of mulled wine and winter spices competes with that of hot waffles and *tartiflette*, a dish from the French Alps made with cheese, potatoes, onions and bacon and one that has become a winter staple in Belgium too.

Come January, the party spirit prevails with New Year being another opportunity for a big family meal. And then, on January 6, Epiphany or Three Kings' Day is celebrated. A culinary tradition associated with this day is the baking of a *galette des Rois* or *driekoningentaart* (literally '(Three) Kings' cake'), in which a bean or a small figurine is placed in the middle. When cut, whoever gets the slice with the bean or figurine becomes King for the day.

ALL YEAR ROUND

Epiphany may well round off the end-of-year festivities, but it isn't long until the partying and feasting starts again with carnival in mid-February. Two Belgian towns that are particularly renowned for their carnival celebrations, which date back hundreds of years, are Aalst in Flanders and Binche in Wallonia. Both UNESCO-recognised events are marked by lavish costumes and take place in the days leading up to Lent. A common feature of carnival throughout Belgium is plenty of eating and drinking: pancakes, waffles, doughnut balls and beer are all consumed in large quantities.

Feasting and merrymaking have been a part of Belgian life for centuries and to this day almost every town and village has its annual fair where eating, drinking and generally having fun are the order of the day. Waffle vans and chip stands compete for custom with food stalls selling everything from candyfloss to sausages. To capture the spirit of the so-called *kermesse* in past centuries, paintings by Brueghel and Teniers are most enlightening: they depict crowds of people armed with tankards, eating, dancing and playing music. Traditionally, the *kermesse* was a fair commemorating the consecration of the local church, with the word a combination of *kerk* meaning church and *messe* meaning mass. In the past, the *kermesse* involved a procession and a fair; in many towns today, it is just the fair that remains.

Special occasions in Belgium are often linked with the cycle of the year, either celebrating an important date in the Christian calendar (Belgium is a predominantly Catholic country) or holding an annual event to observe a local tradition. Yet the cycle of life also provides plenty of occasions to celebrate.

When a baby is born, the parents traditionally give a small packet of sugared and chocolate coated almonds, known as *suikerbonen* in Dutch and *dragées* in French, to friends and family. For a child's first communion, the event is marked in Flanders with an *ijslam*, ice cream in the shape of a lamb that the child cuts into and grenadine juice drips out. Weddings are opportunities for afternoon fine dining with immediate family and evening partying and eating with a wider circle. In short, Belgians are a people who love to eat, drink and party.

Epiphany CAKE

6-8 servings

2 mixing bowls
Clingfilm
1 small bowl
1 small piece of tinfoil

Preparing: 20 minutes
Resting: 3 hours

FOR THE PASTRY:
300g flour
300g butter
120ml cold water
2 tsp white wine vinegar
(or lemon juice)
1 generous pinch of salt
OPTIONAL:
1 tbsp icing sugar
FOR THE FILLING:
120g sugar
120g butter
120g ground almonds
2 eggs
2 tbsp self-raising flour
2 drops almond essence
OPTIONAL:
1 tsp rum
1 almond, butterbean or
porcelain figurine

— Making fresh puff pastry is VERY time (3 hours) and labour-intensive. You can always use the store-bought, pre-rolled variety. To make the pastry yourself, sieve the flour into a bowl in order to aerate it, and add a generous pinch of salt. Mix in 100g of butter then 120ml of cold water and a couple of teaspoons of lemon juice or white wine vinegar. Knead until smooth, then wrap in clingfilm and put in the fridge for half an hour. Make sure that the rest of the butter is out of the fridge as it will need to be soft.

— Take the dough out of the fridge and roll it out on a floured work surface into a rectangle of about 30x40cm. Spread the remaining 200g of soft butter across ⅔ of the dough, and then fold it into 3, like you would a letter, with the section of unbuttered dough being laid over the middle buttered one. The remaining buttered third then goes over the other 2 layers. Roll the pastry out, fold it again in the same letter-like way and then put it in the fridge for half an hour.

— The dough needs to be rolled, folded and refrigerated at least 6 times, so for 3 hours you will need to return to the kitchen every half hour. If the dough is left in the fridge for too long it will become brittle, and if rolled out too frequently, the butter will absorb into the flour and the pastry won't puff up into lots of very thin crispy layers. Set a timer to remind you when the dough is ready for another roll.

FILLING:

— Prepare the filling by mixing 120g of sugar into 120g of very soft butter. Once smooth, stir in 120g of ground almonds (freshly ground in a food processor or shop-bought). Fold in the 2 beaten eggs a third at a time and hold a little back in order to glaze the cake later. Add a couple of drops of almond essence and a teaspoon of rum (optional) to give a deeper flavour. Sieve in the flour and mix together.

PUTTING THE CAKE TOGETHER:

— Roll the pastry out so that it is big enough to cut two circles out of it. Make the bottom one about 25cm in diameter, and the top layer 2cm wider

· · · →

on each side. Place the bottom layer on a greased baking tray and spoon the almond filling onto the pastry to form a small mound that is slightly higher in the middle and reaches out to the edges, leaving a border of 1-2cm. You can now put an almond, bean or figurine inside. Wet the border with water and then cover with the top layer of pastry. Using your hands, gently press down on the top layer to ensure there is no air inside the cake and seal the edges by firmly pressing the pastry together.

— Make a small hole in the middle of the top layer of pastry, and into this, put a small piece of rolled-up tinfoil, about 1cm high and the diameter of a pencil. This is called a chimney and serves to allow steam to escape. Use the back of a knife to decorate the top of the cake: a leaf pattern is traditional.

— Glaze the cake with the remaining beaten egg and put in a pre-heated oven at 220°C for 35 minutes. 5 minutes before the end of the cooking time you can give the cake a shinier glaze by shaking a tablespoon of icing sugar over the top.

A whole almond, dry butterbean or porcelain figurine is put into the cake and whoever finds it in their portion is the king or queen for the day. So serve the cake with a paper crown.

It is traditional that the youngest person at the table should be the one who cuts and distributes the slices of cake.

Christmas LOG

🍴 10-12 servings

🍴 2 saucepans

1 jar

1 milk pan

1 frying pan

1 large mixing bowl

1 rectangular baking tray
(30x40cm)

🕐 Preparation: 1 ½ hour

Refrigeration: min. 2 hours

Assembling: 20 minutes

FOR THE SPECULOOS PASTE:

150g speculoos biscuits

175ml apple juice

50g unsalted butter

1 tsp cornflour

1 tsp finely ground cinnamon

½ lemon

OPTIONAL:

50ml milk

FOR THE WHITE

CHOCOLATE GANACHE:

150g white chocolate

200ml thick cream

200ml mascarpone

FOR THE PINEAPPLE FILLING:

350g pineapple flesh

1 tbsp rum (or cognac)

THE SPECULOOS PASTE:

— Break the speculoos biscuits into crumbs using a food processor or by putting the biscuits in a bag and pounding it with a rolling pin.

— Pour the apple juice into a saucepan with the juice of half a lemon, the cinnamon and the cornflour. If you are using store-bought biscuits, rather than home-made ones [→ see recipe on p.186], compensate for their extra sweetness by replacing 50ml of the apple juice with milk. Give the contents of the pan a stir with a fork to break up of any lumps of spice or cornflour, then add the butter and turn the heat on to a low temperature.

— Stir a few times while the butter is melting. When the butter has turned to liquid, the sauce will begin to thicken. Take the saucepan off the heat and stir in the biscuit crumbs. The mixture will quickly turn into a gluey paste. Transfer to a jar and allow to cool for an hour before putting the lid on and storing in the fridge, where it will keep for a couple of weeks.

THE WHITE CHOCOLATE GANACHE:

— Break the white chocolate into small pieces and place in a milk pan with thick cream. Set to a low heat and stir regularly as the chocolate melts and takes on the consistency and colour of condensed milk. Remove the pan from the heat and when the pan has cooled, cover with clingfilm and refrigerate for a minimum of 2 hours. Later, before covering the cake with this topping, add 200ml of mascarpone and whisk until firm.

THE PINEAPPLE AND SPECULOOS FILLING:

— Chop the 350g of pineapple flesh into very small pieces by hand. Heat the fine pineapple mince in a frying pan over a high heat for about 2 minutes. The aim is not to cook the pineapple but to heat it sufficiently for its excess water to be released. Pour this away, leaving 250g of fruit. To enrich the flavour, you can pour a tablespoon of rum or cognac over the pineapple.

— Stir about ⅔ of a jar of speculoos paste into the pineapple, then leave to cool for at least an hour before use.

· · · →

FOR THE LOG CAKE:

120g sugar

4 very fresh organic eggs

120g plain flour

1 heaped tsp baking powder

1 large knob of butter

2 tbsp water

1 tsp lemon juice

1 tsp vinegar

Decoration of your choice

THE LOG CAKE:

— Line a 30x40cm baking tray with greaseproof paper and rub a large knob of butter into it. Then put a cup of water into a casserole dish and place this on the bottom of your oven, which needs to be pre-heated to 180°C.

— Dissolve 120g of sugar in 3 tablespoons of water in a small saucepan over a low heat. When the sugar has dissolved, pour the liquid into a bowl to cool a little and stir in lemon juice and vinegar.

— Whisk 4 eggs in a large mixing bowl with an electric whisk for 6-7 minutes, until the mixture has tripled in size and a drop of the foam sticks to your finger. The objective when whisking is to get as much air into the mixture as possible.

— After whisking for 5 minutes, add the sugar syrup in a slow steady stream and continue whisking for 2 minutes. Then sieve the flour and a heaped teaspoon of baking powder into the mousse. Do this in small amounts, stirring the flour in with large circular motions, bringing the mousse up from the bottom of the bowl. It is better to use a metal spoon or a plastic spatula rather than a wooden spoon.

— Pour the thick mousse into the baking tray, spread so as to form an even thickness and cook in the middle of an oven at 180°C for around 8-10 minutes. You will know that the cake is ready because when you press down gently with your finger, the cake will spring back and the outline of your finger will disappear, but try not to open the oven unnecessarily.

— When the cake is cooked, remove it from the oven and turn it out onto a damp tea towel or a piece of tinfoil. Carefully peel off the greaseproof paper, then gently roll the cake into a spiral form – including the tea towel or tinfoil. Let the cake cool for an hour or two in this shape.

PUTTING THE LOG TOGETHER:

— When the log has cooled, unroll it sufficiently to remove the tea towel or tin foil. Then spread the pineapple and speculoos paste across its inside. Roll the cake back up, transfer it to a serving plate or a board and cover with the white chocolate ganache.

— The log can be decorated in a seasonal manner or with elements that emphasise the speculoos: a cinnamon stick, some candied ginger, a star anise, half a nutmeg, some cloves and some white peppercorns. Other attractive and tasty decorations include physalis fruit, kumquats, sour cherries, chocolate-coated candied orange peel, roast hazelnuts and almonds, currants, pistachio nuts, nougat and meringue.

— The vinegar and lemon juice will not influence the flavour; they simply react with the baking powder to form carbon dioxide gas bubbles that will add lightness.

— The flavours of this dessert would be complemented by mocha or ginger ice cream.

WORD OF THANKS

We'd like to thank our friends, families and colleagues for their support, be it testing a recipe, loaning us a family cookbook, sharing tips, making suggestions or simply lending an ear. We also want to extend a special thanks to the many chefs and experts we spoke to along the way. And last but not least a big thank you to the editorial team at Luster for giving us the opportunity to write the book. – Anna and Neil

A special thanks from Hilde to Aunt Wies and grandma.

Biographies

ANNA JENKINSON,

an Oxford University graduate with more than 15 years' journalism experience, loves learning about different cultures and understanding what makes them tick. Her writings about life in Belgium have been published in international and local newspapers, in books and on her website *www.annajenkinson.com*.

NEIL EVANS

is passionate about cooking. Having grown up in Belgium, his first culinary experiments were with many of the traditional Belgian dishes found in this book. Over the years he has toured the country and acquired a sizeable collection of Belgian cookbooks dating back more than a century. He tweets *@TastyBelgium*.

DIANE HENDRIKX

has been working as a photographer for 20 years. She is much in demand for her food, interior and lifestyle photographs which have been published by various upmarket magazines, and in several Luster-books, such as *Nostalgie aan zee* (Nostalgia along the North Sea Coast, 2009), *Belgian designers and their interiors* (2011) and *Living in Antwerp* (2012).

HILDE OEYEN

has been cooking since she was a child. She taught herself how to cook, starting from the age of 13, by reading a lot, observing, and trial and error. She now works as a freelance foodstylist for Belgian magazines such as *Vitaya* and for advertising campaigns for brands such as Philapelhia, Knorr and Boursin. She organises workshops and is the author of the cookbooks (in Dutch) *Libelle salades* and *Libelle ovenschotels*.

Photo Credits

All photos by Diane Hendrikx, except for:

p.25 (top), p.26, p.99, p.101, p.116, p.117, p.131 (top),
p.149, p.151, p.158 (top), p.173, p.174:
 © ImageGlobe

p.25 (bottom), p.27, p.73, p.115, p.181,
p.191 (bottom), p.208:
 © WBT – Jean-Paul Remy

p.33, p.93, p.107, p.125, p.132, p.143:
 © Archief Studio 44/ Tony Le Duc

p.53, p.74, p.141, p.142 (top), p.158 (bottom), p.190:
 © Joram Van Holen

p.65:
 © De Veurn' Ambachtse

p.83, p.100, p.131 (bottom), p.157:
 © Ans Brys

p.84:
 © Museum Plantin-Moretus, foto Peter Maes

p.109:
 © Joke Gossé

p.123, p.124:
 © Maison du Tourisme du Pays de Saint-Hubert

p.150 (top):
 © Le Pain Quotidien

p.165 (top), p.166 (bottom):
 © Toerisme Sint-Truiden - Toerisme Limburg

p.166 (top):
 © Sirop de Liège – Siroperie Meurens

p.182, p.207:
 © Maison Dandoy

p.197, p.198:
 © Stokerij Wissels

p.209:
 © WBT – A. Brancart

All cover photos by Diane Hendrikx, except for:

front cover:
 cow: © Joke Gossé
 grande boucherie moderne: © WBT – Jean-Paul Remy

back cover:
 chicken: © Archief Studio 44/ Tony Le Duc
 sirop de liège: © Sirop de Liège – Siroperie Meurens

Colophon

Recipes: Neil Evans
Stories: Anna Jenkinson

Photography: Diane Hendrikx
Food styling: Hilde Oeyen

Graphic design: Joke Gossé

D/2013/12.005/1
ISBN 978 94 6058 0932
NUR 440

© 2013 Luster, Antwerp
www.lusterweb.com
info@lusterweb.com